SQL FOR DATA SCIENCE

Practical Applications for Real-World Data

THOMPSON CARTER

TABLE OF CONTENTS

Introduction

SQL for Data Science: Practical Applications for Real-World Data"

In today's data-driven world, the ability to manage, manipulate, and analyze vast amounts of data has become a fundamental skill in nearly every field. Whether you're working in finance, healthcare, e-commerce, marketing, or any other industry, data plays an increasingly central role in decision-making. This book, *SQL for Data Science: Practical Applications for Real-World Data*, is designed to bridge the gap between theoretical concepts and practical applications of SQL in the context of data science.

SQL (Structured Query Language) has long been the foundation of relational database management systems (RDBMS). It is the most widely used language for querying and managing data in databases, and its relevance has only grown as the amount of data generated worldwide continues to soar. From querying large datasets to transforming data for machine learning, SQL is at the heart of most data science workflows. But despite its ubiquity, many aspiring data scientists struggle to fully understand SQL's potential or how to leverage it effectively in real-world scenarios. This book aims to change that by providing a comprehensive, jargon-free guide to SQL, tailored specifically to data science applications.

The Power of SQL in Data Science

At its core, data science is about understanding and extracting valuable insights from data. To achieve this, data scientists need to be able to access, clean, analyze, and transform data in ways that are efficient, scalable, and meaningful. SQL is the key tool that allows data scientists to do all of this and more. While other programming languages like Python and R are popular for tasks such as statistical modeling, data visualization, and machine learning, SQL remains the go-to tool for managing and querying data stored in relational databases.

SQL is a powerful language that provides data scientists with the ability to retrieve, filter, aggregate, and combine data from multiple sources. It is also instrumental in preparing data for machine learning models, performing exploratory data analysis (EDA), and generating reports. SQL's combination of simplicity and depth makes it an essential skill for any data scientist. This book will not only teach you how to use SQL for querying databases, but also how to apply these skills to real-world data science problems, from data cleaning and transformation to performance optimization and advanced analytics.

Why This Book?

While there are many resources available for learning SQL, *SQL for Data Science: Practical Applications for Real-World Data* is different in a few key ways:

1. **Jargon-Free Approach**: Data science and SQL can be intimidating, especially if you're new to the field or lack a technical background. This book is written with the goal of making complex SQL concepts accessible to everyone. We've stripped away unnecessary jargon and focused on providing clear, concise explanations that are easy to understand, even for beginners.

2. **Real-World Use Cases**: One of the major challenges for aspiring data scientists is understanding how to apply their skills to real-world problems. This book provides practical examples drawn from actual data science projects across a wide variety of industries. Each chapter includes real-world use cases that demonstrate how SQL is used to solve common data-related challenges, from customer analytics and sales reporting to fraud detection and recommendation systems.

3. **Focus on Data Science Applications**: This book is specifically designed for data science. While SQL is a versatile language used in many different contexts, this book emphasizes how SQL can be used to support the entire data science lifecycle—from collecting and cleaning data to building predictive models. You'll learn how to use

SQL to transform raw data into a format suitable for machine learning, create features for predictive models, and optimize queries for performance in large datasets.

4. **Hands-On, Practical Learning**: Learning SQL in isolation is one thing, but learning how to use SQL in the context of data science requires hands-on experience. Each chapter includes practical exercises and examples that encourage active learning. You will work with real datasets to practice writing SQL queries, cleaning and transforming data, performing analytics, and optimizing your workflows.

What You'll Learn

This book is structured to guide you through SQL's core concepts while focusing on its practical applications in data science. Here's an overview of what you can expect to learn:

- **Introduction to SQL**: You'll start by learning what SQL is, how it fits into the data science ecosystem, and why it remains a critical tool for data professionals. We'll explain how SQL relates to other programming languages used in data science, such as Python and R.

- **Setting Up SQL**: Before diving into complex queries, you'll need to know how to set up your SQL environment. We'll guide you through the process of installing MySQL,

PostgreSQL, or SQLite, and introduce you to SQL editors and command-line interfaces.

- **Basic SQL Syntax**: You'll learn how to write basic SQL queries to retrieve data from relational databases. You'll explore essential SQL commands such as SELECT, FROM, WHERE, and ORDER BY.

- **Data Types and Table Structure**: You'll gain a solid understanding of how data is stored in relational databases. This includes creating tables, defining columns, and working with different data types, such as integers, text, and dates.

- **Aggregating Data**: You'll learn how to summarize and aggregate data using functions like COUNT(), SUM(), AVG(), and MIN(). You'll also explore how to group data with the GROUP BY clause and filter grouped results with HAVING.

- **Joins**: One of SQL's most powerful features is the ability to combine data from multiple tables. You'll learn how to use different types of joins—INNER JOIN, LEFT JOIN, and RIGHT JOIN—to link related data and extract meaningful insights.

- **Subqueries and Nested Queries**: You'll discover how to use subqueries and nested queries to solve more complex problems, such as finding customers who made more than the average purchase in a given time frame.

- **Data Cleaning and Transformation**: Data often comes in messy, unstructured formats that need to be cleaned and transformed. You'll learn how to handle missing data, convert data types, and perform transformations to prepare your data for analysis or machine learning.

- **Advanced SQL Functions and Performance Optimization**: You'll delve into more advanced SQL techniques such as window functions, indexing, and query optimization to work with large datasets efficiently.

- **SQL in Cloud Platforms and Big Data**: As data science increasingly moves to the cloud and into Big Data environments, you'll learn how SQL is used in modern cloud platforms like AWS, Google Cloud, and Azure, as well as how SQL interacts with distributed systems.

- **SQL for Machine Learning**: Finally, you'll explore how SQL can be integrated into machine learning workflows to prepare data, create features, and evaluate model performance.

Who This Book Is For

This book is ideal for anyone interested in learning SQL for data science, whether you're just starting out in the field or looking to expand your skill set. It is designed for:

- **Aspiring Data Scientists**: If you're looking to enter the field of data science, this book will equip you with the SQL skills needed to work effectively with data in real-world projects.

- **Data Analysts and Engineers**: Professionals who already have a background in data analysis or engineering but want to sharpen their SQL skills and apply them to data science tasks.

- **Business Analysts**: If you work in a business role and need to extract, analyze, and report on data, this book will help you learn how to leverage SQL for business intelligence tasks.

- **Students and Educators**: If you are learning or teaching data science, this book offers a structured approach to learning SQL that emphasizes practical applications and real-world examples.

Why SQL Matters in Data Science

SQL is the foundation upon which many data-driven applications are built. Whether you're working with structured data, interacting with cloud platforms, or preparing data for machine learning models, SQL is an indispensable tool for data scientists. By mastering SQL, you gain the ability to work with and manipulate data efficiently—an essential skill in today's fast-paced, data-driven world.

In the chapters that follow, you'll discover how to take advantage of SQL's full potential. With practical examples, easy-to-follow explanations, and hands-on exercises, this book will give you the tools to use SQL to its fullest in your data science journey. Let's begin!

Chapter 1: Introduction to SQL and Data Science

Overview of SQL: What is SQL? Why is it essential for Data Science?

SQL (Structured Query Language) is a powerful, domain-specific language used for managing and manipulating relational databases. SQL allows users to interact with databases to retrieve, insert, update, and delete data. As the standard language for relational database management systems (RDBMS) like MySQL, PostgreSQL, and SQL Server, SQL plays a crucial role in data management and is foundational for anyone working with structured data.

SQL is essential for data science for several key reasons:

- **Data Extraction**: Data scientists need to work with large datasets stored in relational databases. SQL enables them to efficiently extract data from these databases through queries.
- **Data Transformation**: SQL provides tools for cleaning, transforming, and aggregating data. This is often the first step in any data science workflow before any modeling or analysis can begin.

- **Data Analysis**: SQL allows for complex querying, including filtering, sorting, grouping, and joining tables. This is critical for summarizing and exploring data, finding patterns, and generating insights.

- **Integration with Other Tools**: SQL is widely compatible with other data science tools like Python, R, and machine learning platforms. Data scientists often use SQL to retrieve data, which is then analyzed or modeled using these tools.

Without SQL, data scientists would struggle to access, clean, or analyze the structured data that drives most of their analyses and models.

Data Science and its Role: How Data is Analyzed and Interpreted Using SQL

Data science is the process of extracting knowledge and insights from data using a combination of statistics, programming, and domain knowledge. One of the core components of data science is working with large volumes of structured data, which often reside in databases.

SQL serves as the bridge between raw data and the analytical processes of data science. Here's how it fits into the data science workflow:

1. **Data Acquisition**: SQL is used to query databases and retrieve relevant data. Whether it's a marketing campaign's performance metrics or historical financial records, SQL is the starting point for data extraction.

2. **Data Cleaning and Preprocessing**: Before data can be analyzed, it often needs to be cleaned and transformed. SQL functions help remove duplicates, handle missing values, convert data types, and perform other preprocessing tasks.

3. **Exploratory Data Analysis (EDA)**: SQL allows data scientists to perform EDA by summarizing datasets using aggregate functions like COUNT, SUM, AVG, and GROUP BY. This helps identify trends, distributions, and anomalies in the data.

4. **Data Aggregation and Summarization**: SQL's ability to group, filter, and aggregate data makes it perfect for summarizing large datasets into meaningful insights. For example, it can quickly calculate average sales by product or determine the total revenue by region.

5. **Preparing Data for Modeling**: Once the data is cleaned and transformed, SQL can be used to create the dataset that will be fed into machine learning algorithms. This could include merging multiple tables, creating derived features, or aggregating data to a higher level (e.g., daily averages).

6. **Reporting and Dashboarding**: SQL is often used to pull data for reports and dashboards. Business analysts rely on SQL to deliver accurate and timely data for business decision-making.

Real-World Example: How SQL is Used in Businesses for Customer Analytics, Financial Reporting, and More

Let's look at some real-world examples of how SQL is used in various business sectors:

- **Customer   Analytics**: A retail company might use SQL to analyze customer behavior on its e-commerce platform. By querying customer data, the company can identify purchasing trends, customer demographics, and product preferences. SQL queries could be used to segment customers based on purchasing frequency, revenue, or geographic location, helping the company tailor marketing campaigns or improve customer retention strategies.

  Example SQL Query:

  ```sql
  Copy code
  SELECT customer_id, COUNT(order_id) AS order_count,
  AVG(order_total) AS avg_spend
  ```

```
FROM orders
GROUP BY customer_id
HAVING order_count > 5;
```

This query identifies customers who have made more than five purchases and calculates their average spend. Insights like this can guide targeted marketing and loyalty programs.

- **Financial**   **Reporting**:
Financial analysts in companies use SQL to generate reports that track revenue, expenses, and profit margins. SQL is ideal for aggregating and summarizing financial data across multiple tables, such as revenue from different departments, sales figures, and costs.

Example SQL Query:

```
sql
Copy code
SELECT department_name, SUM(revenue) AS total_revenue,
SUM(expenses) AS total_expenses
FROM financials
GROUP BY department_name
ORDER BY total_revenue DESC;
```

This query aggregates revenue and expenses for each department in a company, sorting them in descending order to see which departments are most profitable.

- **Healthcare   Analytics**:

  Hospitals and healthcare providers use SQL to analyze patient records, treatment outcomes, and medical costs. For example, a healthcare provider may use SQL to analyze the number of patients who visited for specific treatments, track recovery times, and identify patterns of disease in different demographic groups.

  Example SQL Query:

  sql
  Copy code

  ```
  SELECT    patient_id,    COUNT(visit_id)    AS    visit_count,
  AVG(visit_duration) AS avg_visit_length
  FROM patient_visits
  GROUP BY patient_id
  HAVING visit_count > 3;
  ```

  This query finds patients who have visited the hospital more than three times and calculates their average visit length, useful for analyzing patients with chronic conditions.

- **Marketing   Analytics**:

  In marketing, SQL is used to assess the effectiveness of campaigns, track user behavior on websites, and optimize advertising efforts. Companies use SQL to calculate key metrics such as conversion rates, customer acquisition costs, and return on investment (ROI).

Example SQL Query:

```sql
Copy code
SELECT campaign_name, COUNT(user_id) AS conversions,
SUM(ad_spend) AS total_spent
FROM campaign_data
GROUP BY campaign_name;
```

This query calculates the number of conversions and total ad spend per campaign, enabling marketers to assess the ROI of their efforts.

SQL is the backbone of data manipulation in data science, helping professionals to query, analyze, and interpret data in meaningful ways. Its role in business, healthcare, finance, and marketing shows how versatile and powerful it can be when working with structured data to generate actionable insights.

Chapter 2: Setting Up SQL

Installing SQL Database Systems: How to Set Up MySQL, PostgreSQL, or SQLite

Before you can start working with SQL, you need to install a database system. The three most commonly used SQL databases in data science are MySQL, PostgreSQL, and SQLite. Each has its strengths and use cases, and choosing the right one depends on your needs. In this chapter, we'll cover how to install and set up these three database systems.

---

1. Installing MySQL

MySQL is one of the most widely used relational database management systems (RDBMS). It's known for being fast, reliable, and easy to use, which makes it popular for web applications and data-driven projects.

Steps to install MySQL:

- **Download**: Go to the official MySQL website (https://dev.mysql.com/downloads/) and download the installer for your operating system (Windows, macOS, or Linux).
- **Run the Installer**: Once the download is complete, run the installer. For Windows, select the "MySQL Installer"

(which will install MySQL Server, Workbench, and other tools). For macOS, you can use Homebrew or download the DMG file.

- **Configuration**: During the installation, you'll be prompted to configure your MySQL server. The defaults are fine for most users, but make sure to set a root password, which will be required to log in.

- **Testing the Installation**: Once MySQL is installed, you can test the installation by opening a terminal or command prompt and typing:

```bash
Copy code
mysql -u root -p
```

Enter the root password you set during installation to log into the MySQL shell.

---

2. Installing PostgreSQL

PostgreSQL is an open-source RDBMS known for its advanced features, such as support for JSON, complex queries, and robust concurrency handling. It's widely used in data science, especially for large datasets and applications requiring complex queries.

Steps to install PostgreSQL:

- **Download**: Visit the official PostgreSQL website (https://www.postgresql.org/download/) and select your operating system.
- **Run the Installer**: Download and run the installer. During installation, you'll be asked to choose installation components. Make sure to select "pgAdmin," which is the graphical interface for PostgreSQL.
- **Set Up the Password**: When prompted, set a password for the default PostgreSQL user (postgres).
- **Start PostgreSQL**: After installation, PostgreSQL should start automatically. You can open the command line or pgAdmin to access your database.
- **Testing the Installation**: To test the installation, open a terminal or command prompt and type:

```bash
Copy code
psql -U postgres
```

Enter the password you set earlier to log into the PostgreSQL shell.

---

3. Installing SQLite

SQLite is a lightweight, serverless SQL database engine. It's embedded directly into applications, making it ideal for smaller projects or personal use. It's commonly used for local development, mobile apps, or prototyping.

Steps to install SQLite:

- **Download**: Visit the official SQLite website (https://www.sqlite.org/download.html) and download the precompiled binaries for your operating system.
- **Run the Installer**: For Windows, you'll download a zip file that contains the SQLite executable. For macOS or Linux, you can install SQLite using a package manager (Homebrew for macOS or apt for Linux).
  - For macOS: brew install sqlite
  - For Ubuntu/Linux: sudo apt-get install sqlite3
- **Testing the Installation**: To test SQLite, open a terminal or command prompt and type:

bash
Copy code
sqlite3 test.db

This command will open SQLite and create a new database called test.db.

Tools and Interfaces: Introduction to SQL Editors and Command-Line Interfaces

Once you've installed your SQL database, you'll need an interface to interact with it. There are two main ways to interact with a SQL database:

- **Command-Line Interface (CLI)**: Every SQL database system provides a CLI where you can execute queries directly. While it can be intimidating for beginners, the command-line interface offers powerful, efficient ways to work with databases.

  For MySQL, PostgreSQL, and SQLite, you can use their respective command-line tools to execute SQL commands and manage databases. Here's an overview of each:

  o **MySQL CLI**: After logging in with the mysql command, you can start executing SQL commands. For example:

  ```sql
  Copy code
  CREATE DATABASE my_database;
  USE my_database;
  CREATE TABLE users (id INT, name VARCHAR(100));
  INSERT INTO users (id, name) VALUES (1, 'Alice');
  SELECT * FROM users;
  ```

24

- o **PostgreSQL CLI (psql)**: The PostgreSQL command-line tool is called psql. It works similarly to MySQL, but with a few differences in syntax:

```sql
Copy code
CREATE DATABASE my_database;
\c my_database
CREATE TABLE users (id SERIAL PRIMARY KEY, name VARCHAR(100));
INSERT INTO users (name) VALUES ('Alice');
SELECT * FROM users;
```

- o **SQLite CLI**: SQLite is lightweight, and its CLI operates directly on the database file (e.g., test.db). You can run commands like:

```sql
Copy code
CREATE TABLE users (id INTEGER PRIMARY KEY, name TEXT);
INSERT INTO users (name) VALUES ('Alice');
SELECT * FROM users;
```

- **Graphical User Interfaces (GUIs)**: GUIs are more user-friendly and are often used in production environments, especially by business analysts and non-technical users.
  - o **MySQL Workbench**: MySQL Workbench is an integrated tool for MySQL that includes a query

editor, a data modeling tool, and server management features.

- o **pgAdmin**: pgAdmin is the most popular open-source GUI for PostgreSQL. It allows you to interact with your database via an intuitive web-based interface.
- o **DB Browser for SQLite**: For SQLite, DB Browser for SQLite provides a simple, GUI-based way to manage SQLite databases.

Real-World Example: Setting Up a Local Database for Personal Project Tracking

Let's walk through setting up a simple SQL database for tracking a personal project. Suppose you're building a task management system for your project, where you'll keep track of tasks, deadlines, and priorities.

1. **Choose Your Database**: For a small, local project, SQLite might be the easiest choice because it doesn't require a server, and it works well for personal projects. But if you expect the project to scale or need more advanced features (e.g., concurrency control), PostgreSQL or MySQL might be better.

2. **Install SQLite (or MySQL/PostgreSQL)**: Follow the installation instructions provided earlier. For this example, we'll use SQLite for simplicity.

3. **Create a Database**:

   o Open your terminal and create a new SQLite database called project_tracker.db:

   bash
   Copy code
   ```
   sqlite3 project_tracker.db
   ```

   o This will open the SQLite shell and create the database file.

4. **Create Tables**:

   o Let's create a table for tasks. Each task will have a description, a deadline, and a priority.

   sql
   Copy code
   ```
   CREATE TABLE tasks (
       id INTEGER PRIMARY KEY,
       description TEXT NOT NULL,
       deadline DATE,
       priority INTEGER
   );
   ```

   o This table contains columns for id, description, deadline, and priority.

5. **Insert Data**:

   o Now, let's add some tasks:

   sql
   Copy code
   ```
   INSERT INTO tasks (description, deadline, priority)
   VALUES
       ('Complete project proposal', '2024-12-15', 1),
       ('Design project website', '2024-12-20', 2),
       ('Write final report', '2024-12-25', 3);
   ```

6. **Query Data**:

   o To view all tasks, you can run:

   sql
   Copy code
   ```
   SELECT * FROM tasks;
   ```

   o This will return a list of all tasks in your project, including their descriptions, deadlines, and priorities.

By following these steps, you've set up a local SQL database to track your personal project. This hands-on example shows how SQL can be applied to even small, personal tasks, helping you stay organized and manage your project effectively.

Chapter 3: Basic SQL Syntax and Queries

SELECT Statement: Basic Syntax for Querying Databases

The **SELECT** statement is the most fundamental SQL query used to retrieve data from one or more tables in a database. The basic syntax for using the SELECT statement is as follows:

sql
Copy code
```
SELECT column1, column2, ...
FROM table_name;
```
Here's a breakdown of the syntax:

- **SELECT**: Specifies which columns you want to retrieve.
- **column1, column2, ...**: The columns from which you want to fetch data. If you want to retrieve all columns, you can use the asterisk (*), which is shorthand for all columns.
- **FROM**: Indicates which table to query the data from.
- **table_name**: The name of the table containing the data.

Example:

sql
Copy code
```
SELECT first_name, last_name
```

FROM employees;

This query retrieves the first_name and last_name columns from the employees table. If you wanted to retrieve all columns from the employees table, you could use:

```sql
Copy code
SELECT *
FROM employees;
```

Note: It's important to only select the columns you need, as retrieving unnecessary data (using *) can impact performance, especially with large datasets.

Filtering Data with WHERE: Applying Conditions to Filter Results

To refine the results of your queries, you can use the **WHERE** clause. The **WHERE** clause allows you to specify conditions that must be met for rows to be included in the result set. It's commonly used to filter data based on column values.

The basic syntax for the WHERE clause is:

```sql
Copy code
SELECT column1, column2, ...
FROM table_name
WHERE condition;
```

Conditions in the WHERE clause can involve operators such as:

- **Comparison operators**: =, !=, <, >, <=, >=
- **Logical operators**: AND, OR, NOT
- **Pattern matching**: LIKE
- **Range checking**: BETWEEN
- **NULL checking**: IS NULL, IS NOT NULL

Common Examples of WHERE Clause Usage:

1. **Filtering with Comparison Operators**:

sql
Copy code
```
SELECT first_name, salary
FROM employees
WHERE salary > 50000;
```
This query retrieves the first name and salary of employees whose salary is greater than 50,000.

2. **Filtering with Logical Operators**:

sql
Copy code
```
SELECT first_name, last_name, department
FROM employees
WHERE department = 'Sales' AND salary > 40000;
```
This query retrieves employees who work in the Sales department and have a salary greater than 40,000.

3. **Filtering with LIKE:**

```sql
Copy code
SELECT first_name, last_name
FROM employees
WHERE first_name LIKE 'A%';
```

This query retrieves employees whose first name starts with the letter "A". The % symbol acts as a wildcard to match any sequence of characters.

4. **Filtering with BETWEEN:**

```sql
Copy code
SELECT first_name, hire_date
FROM employees
WHERE hire_date BETWEEN '2020-01-01' AND '2021-01-01';
```

This query retrieves the first name and hire date of employees hired between January 1, 2020, and January 1, 2021.

5. **Filtering with IS NULL:**

```sql
Copy code
SELECT first_name, email
FROM employees
WHERE email IS NULL;
```

This query retrieves employees who do not have an email address (NULL values in the email column).

Real-World Example: Querying a Product Sales Database for Specific Regions and Time Frames

Let's consider a real-world example where you work for an e-commerce company, and you need to query the sales data for products sold in specific regions within a particular time frame.

You have a **sales** table with the following columns:

- **product_id**: Unique identifier for each product.
- **region**: Geographic region where the product was sold (e.g., 'North', 'South', 'East', 'West').
- **sale_date**: Date the sale occurred.
- **sales_amount**: Total amount of the sale.

Your task is to find out the total sales for a specific product in the 'North' and 'South' regions between January 1, 2023, and March 31, 2023.

Query:

```sql
Copy code
SELECT product_id, region, SUM(sales_amount) AS total_sales
FROM sales
```

WHERE region IN ('North', 'South')
 AND sale_date BETWEEN '2023-01-01' AND '2023-03-31'
GROUP BY product_id, region;

Explanation:

- **SELECT product_id, region, SUM(sales_amount) AS total_sales**: This retrieves the product_id, region, and the total sales (SUM(sales_amount)) for each product in the specified regions.
- **FROM sales**: Specifies the table to query data from, which is the sales table in this case.
- **WHERE region IN ('North', 'South')**: Filters the rows to only include sales in the 'North' or 'South' regions.
- **AND sale_date BETWEEN '2023-01-01' AND '2023-03-31'**: Further filters the rows to include sales made between January 1, 2023, and March 31, 2023.
- **GROUP BY product_id, region**: Groups the result set by product_id and region so that we can aggregate the sales for each combination.

This query will return the total sales for each product in the 'North' and 'South' regions within the specified time frame.

Sample Output:

product_id region total_sales

product_id region total_sales

product_id	region	total_sales
101	North	15000
101	South	12000
102	North	18000
102	South	14000

By mastering the SELECT statement and the WHERE clause, you can efficiently query databases, filter data based on specific conditions, and extract meaningful insights for your analysis. In the next chapters, you will learn how to expand on these basic queries by joining tables, performing aggregations, and more.

Chapter 4: Data Types and Table Structure

Understanding Data Types: Integer, Text, Date, etc.

In SQL, data types are crucial because they define the kind of data that can be stored in each column of a table. The choice of data type affects how the data is stored, retrieved, and manipulated. Understanding the most common data types is essential for designing efficient and well-structured databases.

Here are some of the most frequently used SQL data types:

---

1. Integer Data Types

- **INTEGER (INT)**: Stores whole numbers. It's the most common data type for numeric values without decimals.
    - **Example**: Age, quantity, and counts.
    - **Range**: -2,147,483,648 to 2,147,483,647 (for standard INT).
- **SMALLINT**: A smaller integer with a range from -32,768 to 32,767.
    - **Example**: Small numeric values like a rating scale (e.g., 1 to 5).

- **BIGINT**: A larger integer that can store values beyond the range of INT. Typically used when working with large datasets.
  - o **Example**: Population counts, transaction IDs, etc.

2. Decimal and Floating-Point Data Types

- **DECIMAL or NUMERIC**: Stores exact numeric values with fixed decimal places.
  - o **Example**: Monetary values, percentages, and any value requiring exact precision.
  - o **Syntax**: DECIMAL(p, s) where p is the total number of digits and s is the number of digits after the decimal point.
  - o **Example**: DECIMAL(10, 2) would store values like 12345.67.
- **FLOAT**: Stores approximate numeric values with floating decimal points.
  - o **Example**: Scientific calculations, where exact precision is not necessary.
- **DOUBLE PRECISION**: Similar to FLOAT but with a larger range and precision.

3. String Data Types

- **VARCHAR** (Variable-length character string): Stores alphanumeric data. The length of the string can vary, and it's more space-efficient than using a fixed-length string.
  - **Example**: Names, email addresses, descriptions.
  - **Syntax**: VARCHAR(n) where n is the maximum length of the string.
  - **Example**: VARCHAR(255) can store strings up to 255 characters.
- **CHAR** (Fixed-length character string): Stores fixed-length alphanumeric data. If the string is shorter than the defined length, the database will pad it with spaces.
  - **Example**: State codes (e.g., "NY", "CA").
  - **Syntax**: CHAR(n) where n is the fixed length.
- **TEXT**: A variable-length string with no specific upper limit (useful for large text data).
  - **Example**: Long descriptions, product reviews, comments.

---

4. Date and Time Data Types

- **DATE**: Stores calendar dates (year, month, day).
  - **Example**: Birthdate, hire date, transaction date.
  - **Syntax**: YYYY-MM-DD.

   o   **Example**: '2024-12-01'.

- **TIME**: Stores time values (hours, minutes, seconds).

   o   **Example**: Event times, opening hours.

   o   **Syntax**: HH:MM:SS.

   o   **Example**: '13:30:00'.

- **DATETIME**: Stores both date and time in a single column.

   o   **Example**: Timestamp of when a transaction occurred.

   o   **Syntax**: YYYY-MM-DD HH:MM:SS.

   o   **Example**: '2024-12-01 14:30:00'.

- **TIMESTAMP**: Similar to DATETIME, but typically includes information about the time zone and may automatically update when records are modified.

5. Boolean Data Type

- **BOOLEAN**: Stores logical values — TRUE or FALSE.

   o   **Example**: is_active, is_verified.

6. Other Data Types

- **BLOB (Binary Large Object)**: Used for storing binary data such as images, audio files, and documents.

- o **Example**: Storing profile pictures or product images.
- **ENUM**: Stores a list of predefined values.
  - o **Example**: status (e.g., 'Active', 'Inactive', 'Pending').

Creating Tables: Defining Structure with CREATE TABLE

Once you understand the different data types, you can start creating tables to organize your data. The **CREATE TABLE** statement allows you to define the structure of a table, specifying the names, data types, and any constraints for each column.

The basic syntax for creating a table is:

```sql
Copy code
CREATE TABLE table_name (
    column1 datatype constraint,
    column2 datatype constraint,
    ...
);
```

Where:

- **table_name** is the name you give to the table.
- **column1, column2, ...** are the columns in the table.
- **datatype** is the type of data the column will store (e.g., VARCHAR, INTEGER, DATE).

- **constraint** is optional but used to define rules for the data (e.g., NOT NULL, PRIMARY KEY).

Example: Creating a Users Table

Let's create a table called users that holds information about users in a recommendation engine, such as their user_id, first_name, last_name, email, join_date, and is_active status.

sql
Copy code

```
CREATE TABLE users (
    user_id INT PRIMARY KEY,      -- unique identifier for each user
    first_name VARCHAR(100) NOT NULL, -- user's first name
    last_name VARCHAR(100) NOT NULL,  -- user's last name
    email VARCHAR(255) UNIQUE NOT NULL, -- user's email (unique constraint)
    join_date DATE NOT NULL,      -- the date the user joined
    is_active BOOLEAN DEFAULT TRUE   -- status of the user's account, default is TRUE
);
```

Explanation:

- **user_id**: The INT data type is used to store the user's unique identifier, and it is marked as the **PRIMARY KEY** to ensure that each user_id is unique.

- **first_name** and **last_name**: These are both VARCHAR columns with a maximum length of 100 characters, and the NOT NULL constraint ensures that these fields cannot be left empty.

- **email**: This column is also VARCHAR, but it has a UNIQUE constraint to ensure that no two users can have the same email address.

- **join_date**: The DATE data type is used to store the date the user joined the system.

- **is_active**: This is a BOOLEAN column that indicates whether the user's account is active. It has a default value of TRUE, meaning that new users will be active by default unless specified otherwise.

Real-World Example: Building a User Profile Table for a Recommendation Engine

In a recommendation engine, we need a table to store user profiles, which will contain key attributes about each user. The users table can be extended with additional columns to support the recommendation algorithm. These attributes may include preferences, historical data on past interactions, and the type of recommendations that best fit the user.

Here's an example of how you might expand the users table:

sql

Copy code

```sql
CREATE TABLE user_profiles (
    user_id INT PRIMARY KEY,
    first_name VARCHAR(100) NOT NULL,
    last_name VARCHAR(100) NOT NULL,
    email VARCHAR(255) UNIQUE NOT NULL,
    join_date DATE NOT NULL,
    is_active BOOLEAN DEFAULT TRUE,
    preference VARCHAR(255),      -- stores user preferences (e.g., genre, style)
    last_login TIMESTAMP,         -- stores the timestamp of the last login
    total_spent DECIMAL(10, 2),   -- total amount spent by the user
    recommendations_sent INT DEFAULT 0 -- the number of recommendations sent
);
```

Explanation:

- **preference**: A VARCHAR field that can store the user's preference for personalized recommendations (e.g., product type, genre, etc.).
- **last_login**: A TIMESTAMP field to track when the user last interacted with the system.
- **total_spent**: A DECIMAL(10, 2) field that stores the total amount of money the user has spent.
- **recommendations_sent**: An INT field to keep track of how many recommendations have been sent to the user.

By structuring this table efficiently and choosing appropriate data types, you create a robust foundation for building personalized recommendations based on the user profile.

Understanding data types and how to structure your tables is fundamental to building efficient databases. By using the right data types, you ensure that your data is stored accurately and optimally, making it easier to query and manipulate. The ability to create tables with meaningful relationships and constraints sets the stage for more complex queries and analytics, which are key components of data science.

In the next chapter, you will learn about more advanced table structures, including relationships between tables using **primary keys** and **foreign keys**, and how to maintain data integrity with constraints.

Chapter 5: Aggregating Data with SQL

Using COUNT, SUM, AVG, MIN, MAX: How to Aggregate Data for Analysis

In SQL, **aggregation functions** are used to perform calculations on a set of values, which allows you to analyze and summarize your data. These functions are essential for gaining insights from large datasets. Here are the most commonly used aggregation functions:

1. COUNT()

The **COUNT()** function is used to count the number of rows in a dataset or the number of non-NULL values in a specific column.

- **Syntax**:

```sql
Copy code
COUNT(column_name)
```

- **Example**: Counting the total number of orders in the orders table:

```sql
Copy code
```

SQL FOR DATA SCIENCE

SELECT COUNT(order_id) FROM orders;

- **COUNT(*)**: When you don't specify a column, COUNT(*) counts all rows, regardless of whether they contain NULL values.
- **Example**: Counting the total number of rows in the orders table:

sql
Copy code
SELECT COUNT(*) FROM orders;

---

2. SUM()

The **SUM()** function calculates the total sum of a numeric column.

- **Syntax**:

sql
Copy code
SUM(column_name)

- **Example**: Summing the total sales from the sales_amount column in the sales table:

sql
Copy code
SELECT SUM(sales_amount) FROM sales;

---

3. AVG()

The **AVG()** function calculates the average value of a numeric column.

- **Syntax**:

  sql
  Copy code
  AVG(column_name)

- **Example**: Calculating the average sales amount in the sales table:

  sql
  Copy code
  SELECT AVG(sales_amount) FROM sales;

---

4. MIN() and MAX()

The **MIN()** function returns the minimum value in a column, while **MAX()** returns the maximum value.

- **Syntax**:

  sql
  Copy code
  MIN(column_name)
  MAX(column_name)

- **Example**: Finding the minimum and maximum sales amounts in the sales table:

```sql
Copy code
SELECT MIN(sales_amount), MAX(sales_amount) FROM sales;
```

GROUP BY and HAVING: Grouping Data and Filtering Grouped Results

When performing aggregation, you often want to group data by specific criteria, such as by product category or region. The **GROUP BY** clause is used to group rows based on one or more columns. After grouping the data, you can then aggregate it using functions like COUNT(), SUM(), AVG(), etc.

1. GROUP BY

The **GROUP BY** clause groups rows that have the same values into summary rows, like "total sales by region" or "average salary by department."

- **Syntax**:

```sql
Copy code
SELECT column_name, aggregate_function(column_name)
FROM table_name
GROUP BY column_name;
```

- **Example**: Finding the total sales for each region:

sql
Copy code
```
SELECT region, SUM(sales_amount) AS total_sales
FROM sales
GROUP BY region;
```
This query groups the data by the region column and calculates the total sales for each region.

---

2. HAVING

The **HAVING** clause is used to filter groups after the aggregation has been performed, unlike the **WHERE** clause, which filters rows before aggregation. It's essential when you want to filter results based on the aggregated data (e.g., filtering out groups with sales below a certain threshold).

- **Syntax**:

sql
Copy code
```
SELECT column_name, aggregate_function(column_name)
FROM table_name
GROUP BY column_name
HAVING condition;
```

- **Example**: Finding regions with total sales greater than $10,000:

```sql
Copy code
SELECT region, SUM(sales_amount) AS total_sales
FROM sales
GROUP BY region
HAVING SUM(sales_amount) > 10000;
```

In this query, the data is first grouped by region, then aggregated to find the total sales, and the HAVING clause filters out any groups where the total sales are less than $10,000.

Real-World Example: Summarizing Sales Data by Product Categories

Let's look at a real-world example in which you need to analyze sales data by product category. Imagine you work for a retail company, and you want to know the total sales and the average sales amount for each product category.

You have a **sales** table with the following columns:

- product_id: The unique identifier for each product.
- category: The product's category (e.g., 'Electronics', 'Clothing', 'Groceries').
- sales_amount: The amount of each sale.

- sale_date: The date when the sale occurred.

Step 1: Total Sales by Category

To find the total sales for each product category, you would use the SUM() function in combination with the GROUP BY clause:

```sql
Copy code
SELECT category, SUM(sales_amount) AS total_sales
FROM sales
GROUP BY category;
```

Step 2: Average Sales by Category

To find the average sales for each category, you would use the AVG() function with GROUP BY:

```sql
Copy code
SELECT category, AVG(sales_amount) AS avg_sales
FROM sales
GROUP BY category;
```

Step 3: Filtering Categories with High Sales

Now, if you only want to focus on product categories where total sales exceed $50,000, you can use the HAVING clause:

```sql
Copy code
SELECT category, SUM(sales_amount) AS total_sales
FROM sales
GROUP BY category
```

HAVING SUM(sales_amount) > 50000;

This query groups the data by category, calculates the total sales for each category, and then filters the results to show only categories with total sales greater than $50,000.

Sample Output for Total Sales by Category:

category	total_sales
Electronics	120,000
Clothing	45,000
Groceries	75,000

Aggregating data with SQL is a powerful way to analyze and summarize information. By using functions like **COUNT()**, **SUM()**, **AVG()**, **MIN()**, and **MAX()**, you can quickly extract valuable insights from your data. **GROUP BY** enables you to group your data by specific attributes, while **HAVING** allows you to filter those groups based on aggregated results.

In the next chapter, you will learn about **JOINs** and how to combine data from multiple tables to enhance your analysis. This will help you work with more complex databases and perform advanced queries for even deeper insights.

Chapter 6: Joins: Combining Tables

INNER JOIN, LEFT JOIN, RIGHT JOIN: Different Types of Joins and When to Use Them

One of the most powerful features of SQL is the ability to **combine** data from multiple tables using **joins**. Joins allow you to retrieve related data from different tables and combine it into a single result set. This is essential when working with normalized databases, where data is spread across several tables.

There are several types of joins in SQL, each with its own use case. Let's explore the three most common types: **INNER JOIN**, **LEFT JOIN**, and **RIGHT JOIN**.

1. INNER JOIN

An **INNER JOIN** returns only the rows that have matching values in both tables. If there is no match between the tables, the row is excluded from the result.

- **Syntax**:

```
sql
Copy code
SELECT column_name(s)
FROM table1
INNER JOIN table2
```

ON table1.column_name = table2.column_name;

- **Example**: Let's say we have two tables: customers and orders. We want to retrieve a list of customers who have placed an order. Using an **INNER JOIN**, we can combine both tables based on the customer_id column, which is common to both.

sql
Copy code
```
SELECT          customers.customer_id,          customers.first_name,
customers.last_name, orders.order_id, orders.order_date
FROM customers
INNER JOIN orders
ON customers.customer_id = orders.customer_id;
```
In this query, the result will only include customers who have placed at least one order.

---

2. LEFT JOIN (or LEFT OUTER JOIN)

A **LEFT JOIN** returns all the rows from the left table (the table before the JOIN keyword) and the matched rows from the right table (the table after the JOIN keyword). If there is no match, the result will still include the row from the left table, but the columns from the right table will contain **NULL**.

- **Syntax**:

sql

```
Copy code
SELECT column_name(s)
FROM table1
LEFT JOIN table2
ON table1.column_name = table2.column_name;
```

- **Example**: Let's say you want to retrieve a list of all customers, whether or not they have placed an order. This time, we'll use a **LEFT JOIN** to ensure that even customers with no orders are included in the results.

```
sql
Copy code
SELECT           customers.customer_id,           customers.first_name,
customers.last_name, orders.order_id
FROM customers
LEFT JOIN orders
ON customers.customer_id = orders.customer_id;
```

In this query, all customers are listed, and for customers without orders, the order_id will be NULL.

---

3. RIGHT JOIN (or RIGHT OUTER JOIN)

A **RIGHT JOIN** is the opposite of a **LEFT JOIN**. It returns all the rows from the right table and the matched rows from the left table. If there is no match, the result will still include the row from the right table, but the columns from the left table will contain **NULL**.

- **Syntax**:

```sql
Copy code
SELECT column_name(s)
FROM table1
RIGHT JOIN table2
ON table1.column_name = table2.column_name;
```

- **Example**: Using a **RIGHT JOIN** can be useful when you want to return all the rows from the right table. For example, if you want to see all orders (even those that don't have a matching customer in the customers table), you can use a **RIGHT JOIN**.

```sql
Copy code
SELECT      customers.customer_id,      customers.first_name,
customers.last_name, orders.order_id
FROM customers
RIGHT JOIN orders
ON customers.customer_id = orders.customer_id;
```

In this query, every order is listed, and for orders that don't have a corresponding customer (perhaps due to data integrity issues), the customer information will be NULL.

Using JOINs to Link Tables: How Joins Connect Related Data

In relational databases, data is often split across multiple tables. To get meaningful information, you need to combine data from these tables. Joins allow you to link related data across different tables.

- **Example Scenario**: You have two tables:
  - **customers**: Contains customer details.
  - **orders**: Contains order information, with each order linked to a customer via the customer_id field.

By using joins, you can easily retrieve related data across these two tables. For example, you may want to list each customer alongside their order details, such as the order_id and order_date.

Real-World Example: Combining Customer and Order Tables to Analyze Purchase History

Imagine you are analyzing purchase history for customers in an e-commerce business. You have the following two tables:

- **customers** table:
  - customer_id (Primary Key)
  - first_name
  - last_name
  - email
- **orders** table:
  - order_id (Primary Key)
  - customer_id (Foreign Key)

- o   order_date
- o   order_total

Step 1: List all customers and their orders (INNER JOIN)

You want to see a list of all customers who have made purchases, along with the details of their orders. You would use an **INNER JOIN** to return only those customers who have matching records in the orders table.

sql
Copy code
SELECT customers.customer_id, customers.first_name, customers.last_name, orders.order_id, orders.order_date, orders.order_total
FROM customers
INNER JOIN orders
ON customers.customer_id = orders.customer_id;

- **Output**: The result would list customers with their corresponding order_id, order_date, and order_total values, but it will exclude any customers who have not placed any orders.

Step 2: List all customers, even if they haven't made a purchase (LEFT JOIN)

Now, you want to see a list of all customers, including those who have not made any purchases. You would use a **LEFT JOIN** to ensure that all customers are included, and for those who haven't made any orders, the order_id, order_date, and order_total columns will contain NULL values.

sql
Copy code

```
SELECT customers.customer_id, customers.first_name, customers.last_name,
orders.order_id, orders.order_date, orders.order_total
FROM customers
LEFT JOIN orders
ON customers.customer_id = orders.customer_id;
```

- **Output**: This query will return all customers, including those without orders. For customers who have made purchases, you'll see their order details. For customers who haven't made any purchases, the order columns will be NULL.

Step 3: Find all orders, even if the customer is missing (RIGHT JOIN)

In some cases, you might want to see all orders, even if a corresponding customer record is missing. This can occur due to data inconsistencies. A **RIGHT JOIN** will return all orders, and for orders without a matching customer, the customer details will be NULL.

sql
Copy code

```
SELECT customers.customer_id, customers.first_name, customers.last_name,
orders.order_id, orders.order_date, orders.order_total
FROM customers
RIGHT JOIN orders
ON customers.customer_id = orders.customer_id;
```

- **Output**: The result will show all orders, even those that do not have a corresponding customer. If a customer record is missing for any order, the customer columns will be NULL.

Joins are a powerful tool for combining data from different tables in SQL. Understanding the different types of joins—**INNER JOIN, LEFT JOIN**, and **RIGHT JOIN**—is essential for linking related data and performing meaningful analysis. By choosing the appropriate type of join based on your requirements, you can tailor your queries to return the exact data you need.

In the next chapter, we will dive into **subqueries**, which allow you to nest queries within queries to solve more complex problems, enabling even deeper insights into your data.

Chapter 7: Subqueries and Nested Queries

What Are Subqueries? Using Queries Inside Other Queries

A **subquery** is a query that is embedded within another query. Subqueries allow you to break down complex problems into simpler, more manageable parts by enabling you to perform operations like filtering, aggregation, and comparisons in one query and then passing that result to another.

In SQL, subqueries are often used to:

1. Filter results based on the results of another query.
2. Compare a value to a set of values from another query.
3. Perform complex calculations that require intermediate steps.

A **nested query** is essentially a query that appears inside another query, typically within the WHERE, HAVING, FROM, or SELECT clauses.

Types of Subqueries: Correlated vs. Non-Correlated Subqueries

There are two main types of subqueries:

1. **Non-Correlated Subqueries**

2. Correlated Subqueries

1. Non-Correlated Subqueries

A **non-correlated subquery** is a subquery that can be executed independently of the outer query. It does not reference any columns from the outer query. The subquery runs once and the result is used by the outer query.

- **Syntax**:

```sql
Copy code
SELECT column_name
FROM table
WHERE column_name operator (SELECT column_name FROM table
WHERE condition);
```

- **Example**: Suppose you want to find employees who earn more than the average salary in a company. A non-correlated subquery can be used to calculate the average salary and compare it with individual employee salaries.

```sql
Copy code
SELECT employee_name, salary
FROM employees
WHERE salary > (SELECT AVG(salary) FROM employees);
```

Here, the inner query calculates the average salary for all employees. The outer query retrieves the names and salaries of employees who earn more than that average.

2. Correlated Subqueries

A **correlated subquery** is a subquery that refers to a column from the outer query. The inner query cannot be executed independently, as it depends on the outer query's current row. The subquery is evaluated once for each row processed by the outer query.

- **Syntax**:

```
sql
Copy code
SELECT column_name
FROM table1
WHERE column_name operator (SELECT column_name FROM table2 WHERE table1.column_name = table2.column_name);
```

- **Example**: Suppose you want to find customers who have made more purchases than the average number of purchases made by all customers. Since each customer's purchases are compared to the average of all customers, this is a correlated subquery.

```
sql
Copy code
SELECT customer_name
FROM customers c
```

WHERE (SELECT COUNT(*) FROM orders o WHERE o.customer_id = c.customer_id) >

(SELECT AVG(total_orders) FROM (SELECT COUNT(*) AS total_orders FROM orders GROUP BY customer_id) AS avg_orders);

In this example, the subquery depends on the outer query's customer_id to count the number of orders for each customer and then compares it to the overall average number of orders made by customers.

Real-World Example: Finding Customers Who Made More Than the Average Purchase in a Given Month

Let's say you work in the marketing department of an e-commerce company and you want to find all customers who made purchases greater than the average purchase amount in a specific month. You have the following tables:

- **customers:**
  - customer_id (Primary Key)
  - first_name
  - last_name
- **orders:**
  - order_id (Primary Key)
  - customer_id (Foreign Key)
  - order_date
  - order_total

You want to find customers whose total purchase for a given month exceeds the average order total for that month.

Step 1: Calculate the Average Purchase Total for the Month

The first part of this query will calculate the average purchase total for a specific month, using the AVG() function and filtering the order_date by month.

sql
Copy code
```
SELECT AVG(order_total) AS avg_purchase
FROM orders
WHERE MONTH(order_date) = 6 AND YEAR(order_date) = 2024;
```
This query will return the average purchase total for all orders made in June 2024.

Step 2: Find Customers with Purchases Greater Than the Average

Now, to find the customers who made purchases greater than this average, you can use a **subquery**. You'll compare each customer's order_total for the month with the result of the subquery that calculates the average order total.

sql
Copy code
```
SELECT c.customer_id, c.first_name, c.last_name
FROM customers c
WHERE (SELECT SUM(o.order_total)
    FROM orders o
```

```
WHERE o.customer_id = c.customer_id
AND MONTH(o.order_date) = 6
AND YEAR(o.order_date) = 2024) >
(SELECT AVG(order_total)
FROM orders
WHERE MONTH(order_date) = 6 AND YEAR(order_date) = 2024);
```

Explanation:

- The outer query retrieves the customer_id, first_name, and last_name for each customer.
- The inner subquery calculates the total purchase amount for each customer (SUM(o.order_total)) in June 2024.
- The second subquery calculates the average order total for the month of June 2024.
- The WHERE clause in the outer query compares each customer's total purchase against the average, returning only those customers who spent more than the average.

Subqueries in SELECT and FROM Clauses

Subqueries can also be used in the **SELECT** and **FROM** clauses.

- **Using a Subquery in the SELECT Clause**: Sometimes, you might want to return the result of a subquery as a column in your result set. For example, you could calculate the total sales for each customer within the query.

```
sql
Copy code
SELECT c.customer_id, c.first_name, c.last_name,
    (SELECT SUM(order_total) FROM orders WHERE customer_id
= c.customer_id) AS total_spent
FROM customers c;
```

- **Using a Subquery in the FROM Clause**: You can use subqueries in the **FROM** clause to treat the result of a query as a temporary table. For example, you might want to calculate the total sales per customer and then filter those customers who have made total purchases greater than a certain amount.

```
sql
Copy code
SELECT customer_id, total_spent
FROM (SELECT customer_id, SUM(order_total) AS total_spent
    FROM orders
    GROUP BY customer_id) AS sales
WHERE total_spent > 500;
```

Subqueries are a powerful tool in SQL for solving complex problems by allowing you to nest one query within another. They enable you to perform calculations, filtering, and comparisons that would otherwise be difficult to express in a single query. Understanding the difference between **correlated** and **non-**

correlated subqueries is crucial, as it helps you choose the right approach for your data analysis needs.

In the next chapter, we will explore **indexes** and **optimization techniques** to help you make your SQL queries faster and more efficient, especially when dealing with large datasets.

Chapter 8: Data Cleaning and Transformation

Handling Missing Data: Using NULL and IS NULL

Data cleaning is an essential part of data science, as raw data often contains missing or incomplete values. SQL provides tools to help you identify and handle missing data efficiently. In SQL, missing or undefined values are represented by NULL.

What is NULL?

- **NULL** in SQL is a special marker used to indicate that a data value is missing or undefined.
- NULL is **not** the same as an empty string ("") or zero (0). It represents the absence of any value.
- When you query data that includes NULL values, it is important to handle them explicitly.

Handling NULL Values in SQL

1. **Using IS NULL and IS NOT NULL:**
   - To check for NULL values, use the IS NULL condition.
   - To check for values that are not NULL, use the IS NOT NULL condition.

o **Example**: Find all customers who have not provided an email address (NULL value in the email field).

sql
Copy code
SELECT customer_id, first_name, last_name
FROM customers
WHERE email IS NULL;

o **Example**: Find all customers who have provided an email address (non-NULL value in the email field).

sql
Copy code
SELECT customer_id, first_name, last_name
FROM customers
WHERE email IS NOT NULL;

2. **Replacing NULL Values**:

o You may want to replace NULL values with a default value (like 0 or an empty string). SQL provides the COALESCE() function, which returns the first non-NULL value in a list of expressions.

o Alternatively, you can use the IFNULL() function in some SQL databases.

o **Example**: Replace NULL values in the phone_number column with 'N/A'.

```sql
Copy code
SELECT customer_id, first_name, last_name,
       COALESCE(phone_number, 'N/A') AS phone_number
FROM customers;
```

3. **Updating NULL Values**:
   - You can also **update** NULL values in the database with specific values. Use the UPDATE statement with SET to replace NULL values.
   - **Example**: Update customers with NULL email addresses to a placeholder email.

```sql
Copy code
UPDATE customers
SET email = 'noemail@example.com'
WHERE email IS NULL;
```

Data Transformation with SQL Functions: CAST, CONCAT, and More

Data transformation involves converting data from one format or structure to another. SQL provides several built-in functions to help with these tasks, such as type casting, string manipulation, and more.

1. CAST and CONVERT Functions

The CAST() and CONVERT() functions allow you to change the data type of a value. This is useful when you need to perform operations on data in different formats, like converting a string to an integer or a date to a string.

- **CAST() Syntax**:

```sql
Copy code
CAST(expression AS target_data_type)
```

- **CONVERT() Syntax** (available in some databases like SQL Server):

```sql
Copy code
CONVERT(target_data_type, expression)
```

- **Example 1: Converting a string to a number**: You may have a price column stored as a string (e.g., '1000'), and you need to treat it as a numeric value for calculations.

```sql
Copy code
SELECT CAST(price AS DECIMAL(10, 2)) AS price_numeric
FROM products;
```

- **Example 2: Converting a date stored as a string to a date type**: If the order_date is stored as a string but you want to perform date-related operations (e.g., filtering by month), you can cast it to a date type.

sql
Copy code
```
SELECT CAST(order_date AS DATE) AS order_date_transformed
FROM orders;
```

2. String Functions: CONCAT and LENGTH

String manipulation is another common task in data cleaning and transformation. SQL provides a range of string functions to perform operations like concatenation, trimming, and finding the length of a string.

- **CONCAT() Function**: The CONCAT() function concatenates two or more strings into a single string.
  - **Syntax**:

    sql
    Copy code
    ```
    CONCAT(string1, string2, ...)
    ```

  - **Example: Combining first and last names**: Suppose you want to create a full name for customers by concatenating the first_name and last_name fields.

    sql
    Copy code

```sql
SELECT customer_id, CONCAT(first_name, ' ', last_name)
AS full_name
FROM customers;
```

- **LENGTH() Function**: The LENGTH() function returns the length of a string.
    - **Syntax**:

    ```
    sql
    Copy code
    LENGTH(string)
    ```

    - **Example: Checking the length of email addresses**: You might want to ensure that all email addresses have a certain length, for example, checking for invalid emails.

    ```
    sql
    Copy code
    SELECT email, LENGTH(email) AS email_length
    FROM customers
    WHERE LENGTH(email) < 5;
    ```

3. Date Functions: DATE_ADD, DATE_FORMAT

Date handling is a common task in data transformation, especially when working with time-series data. SQL provides several functions to manipulate dates.

- **DATE_ADD() Function**: The DATE_ADD() function adds a specified number of days to a date.
  - **Syntax**:

    ```sql
    Copy code
    DATE_ADD(date, INTERVAL number_of_days DAY)
    ```

  - **Example: Adding 30 days to an order date**: Suppose you want to calculate the delivery date, which is 30 days after the order date.

    ```sql
    Copy code
    SELECT order_id, order_date, DATE_ADD(order_date, INTERVAL 30 DAY) AS delivery_date
    FROM orders;
    ```

- **DATE_FORMAT() Function**: The DATE_FORMAT() function allows you to format a date into a specified format.
  - **Syntax**:

    ```sql
    Copy code
    DATE_FORMAT(date, 'format_string')
    ```

  - **Example: Formatting a date as YYYY-MM-DD**: If you want to display the order_date in a more readable format.

```
sql
Copy code
SELECT order_id, DATE_FORMAT(order_date, '%Y-%m-
%d') AS formatted_order_date
FROM orders;
```

Real-World Example: Cleaning Raw Survey Data for Analysis

Suppose you have a raw survey dataset that contains incomplete, incorrect, and inconsistent data. The survey data is stored in a table called survey_responses, with the following columns:

- respondent_id (ID of the respondent)
- age (Age of the respondent, which may contain NULL values)
- response (Survey response, which may have extra spaces)
- survey_date (Date of the survey response, stored as a string)

Step 1: Handle Missing Age Data

You want to replace the NULL values in the age column with a default value (e.g., 0 or "Unknown").

```
sql
Copy code
UPDATE survey_responses
SET age = 0
WHERE age IS NULL;
```

Step 2: Clean the response Column by Removing Extra Spaces

Survey responses may have leading or trailing spaces, which can make the data inconsistent. You can use the TRIM() function to remove unwanted spaces.

sql
Copy code

```
UPDATE survey_responses
SET response = TRIM(response);
```

Step 3: Convert Survey Date to a Standard Format

The survey_date column is stored as a string, but you want to convert it into a proper DATE format for easier analysis.

sql
Copy code

```
UPDATE survey_responses
SET survey_date = STR_TO_DATE(survey_date, '%Y-%m-%d')
WHERE survey_date IS NOT NULL;
```

Step 4: Remove Invalid Age Entries

Sometimes, there may be invalid age entries (e.g., negative numbers). You can clean this by setting those rows to NULL or replacing them with a valid default value.

sql
Copy code

```
UPDATE survey_responses
SET age = NULL
WHERE age < 0;
```

Data cleaning and transformation are fundamental steps in preparing data for analysis. SQL provides a wide range of functions and techniques to handle missing data, convert data types, manipulate strings, and process dates. By using these tools effectively, you can ensure that your data is clean, consistent, and ready for analysis.

In the next chapter, we will dive into **advanced SQL techniques** like window functions and common table expressions (CTEs) that allow you to perform complex calculations and analysis across rows of data.

Chapter 9: Advanced SQL Functions

Window Functions: ROW_NUMBER(), RANK(), LEAD(), LAG()
Window functions are a powerful set of tools in SQL that allow you to perform calculations across a set of rows related to the current row without collapsing the result set. These functions are especially useful for performing **ranking**, **running totals**, **moving averages**, and other advanced analytical tasks.

Unlike aggregate functions (such as SUM() or AVG()) that group rows together, window functions retain the original row structure and perform operations over a "window" of rows. The window is defined by the **OVER()** clause, which specifies how rows are grouped and ordered.

---

1. ROW_NUMBER() Function

The ROW_NUMBER() function assigns a unique number to each row in the result set. The numbering is based on the order specified by the ORDER BY clause within the OVER() function.

- **Syntax**:

    sql
    Copy code

ROW_NUMBER() OVER (PARTITION BY column1 ORDER BY column2)

- **Example**: Assigning row numbers to products based on their sales, ordered by highest sales first:

sql
Copy code
```
SELECT product_id, product_name, sales,
    ROW_NUMBER() OVER (ORDER BY sales DESC) AS rank
FROM products;
```
This query will assign a unique rank to each product, with the highest-selling product getting the rank 1.

---

2. RANK() Function

The RANK() function works similarly to ROW_NUMBER(), but it allows for tied ranks. If two rows have the same value, they receive the same rank, but the next rank in sequence is skipped (i.e., there will be a gap in the ranking).

- **Syntax**:

sql
Copy code
```
RANK() OVER (PARTITION BY column1 ORDER BY column2)
```

- **Example**: Ranking employees based on their performance scores, allowing for ties:

sql

Copy code

```
SELECT employee_id, employee_name, performance_score,
    RANK() OVER (ORDER BY performance_score DESC) AS rank
FROM employees;
```

If two employees have the same highest performance score, they will both get rank 1, and the next employee will receive rank 3.

---

3. LEAD() and LAG() Functions

The LEAD() and LAG() functions allow you to access data from subsequent or previous rows within the same result set, respectively. These functions are useful for calculating **differences** between consecutive rows (like comparing sales this month to last month) or **trends** over time.

- **LEAD()** returns the value from the next row.
- **LAG()** returns the value from the previous row.

Both functions are typically used in financial or time-series data analysis.

- **Syntax**:

sql

Copy code

LEAD(column, offset) OVER (PARTITION BY column1 ORDER BY column2)

LAG(column, offset) OVER (PARTITION BY column1 ORDER BY column2)

- **Example 1: LEAD()**: Calculate the difference in sales between the current month and the next month.

sql
Copy code
```
SELECT product_id, sales_month, sales,
    LEAD(sales) OVER (PARTITION BY product_id ORDER BY sales_month) AS next_month_sales,
    LEAD(sales) OVER (PARTITION BY product_id ORDER BY sales_month) - sales AS sales_difference
FROM product_sales;
```

In this query, the LEAD() function fetches the sales value for the next month, and the sales_difference column calculates the difference in sales between the current and next months.

- **Example 2: LAG()**: Calculate the difference in sales between the current month and the previous month.

sql
Copy code
```
SELECT product_id, sales_month, sales,
    LAG(sales) OVER (PARTITION BY product_id ORDER BY sales_month) AS previous_month_sales,
    sales - LAG(sales) OVER (PARTITION BY product_id ORDER BY sales_month) AS sales_difference
```

FROM product_sales;

This query uses the LAG() function to fetch the previous month's sales and calculate the difference.

Using Window Functions for Data Analysis

Window functions are invaluable when performing **time-series analysis**, **ranking**, or **calculating moving averages**. They allow you to access different parts of your data set while preserving the granularity of the original data.

Example 1: Running Total with SUM() and Window Functions

A **running total** is a cumulative sum of a particular field, calculated as you move through the data. This is commonly used in sales data, financial statements, or any situation where you need to track the cumulative value over time.

sql
Copy code

```
SELECT sales_month, product_id, sales,
    SUM(sales) OVER (PARTITION BY product_id ORDER BY sales_month) AS running_total
FROM product_sales;
```

In this example:

- SUM(sales) OVER (PARTITION BY product_id ORDER BY sales_month) calculates the cumulative sum of sales for each product, ordered by month.

- This gives you the total sales for each product up to and including the current month.

Example 2: Moving Average with AVG() and Window Functions

A **moving average** is used to smooth out short-term fluctuations in data and highlight longer-term trends. This is often used in stock price analysis, weather forecasting, or financial forecasting.

sql
Copy code
```
SELECT sales_month, product_id, sales,
    AVG(sales) OVER (PARTITION BY product_id ORDER BY sales_month
ROWS BETWEEN 2 PRECEDING AND CURRENT ROW) AS moving_avg
FROM product_sales;
```
In this query:

- AVG(sales) OVER (PARTITION BY product_id ORDER BY sales_month ROWS BETWEEN 2 PRECEDING AND CURRENT ROW) calculates the average sales for the current month and the two preceding months, giving you a moving average.
- The ROWS BETWEEN 2 PRECEDING AND CURRENT ROW defines the window size as the current row and the two previous rows.

Real-World Example: Ranking Products Based on Sales Performance Over Time

Imagine you are analyzing the performance of different products in an e-commerce company over the last year. You want to rank the products based on their **monthly sales performance** and identify the top-selling products each month.

- **Tables**:
  - **products**: Contains product details.
    - product_id, product_name
  - **product_sales**: Contains sales data for each product by month.
    - product_id, sales_month, sales

Step 1: Rank Products by Sales Performance Each Month

You can use the RANK() function to assign ranks to the products based on their sales for each month.

sql
Copy code
```
SELECT product_id, sales_month, sales,
    RANK() OVER (PARTITION BY sales_month ORDER BY sales DESC) AS monthly_rank
FROM product_sales;
```

This query will return a list of products ranked by their sales within each month. Products with the highest sales will be ranked first. If two products have the same sales value, they will receive the same rank.

Step 2: Identify the Top-Performing Products Over Time

You can use the ROW_NUMBER() function to find the top-performing product in each month.

```sql
Copy code
SELECT product_id, sales_month, sales,
    ROW_NUMBER() OVER (PARTITION BY sales_month ORDER BY sales DESC) AS top_product_rank
FROM product_sales
WHERE ROW_NUMBER() OVER (PARTITION BY sales_month ORDER BY sales DESC) = 1;
```

This query will give you the top-selling product for each month, where ROW_NUMBER() assigns a unique rank to each product within the month. The WHERE clause filters to show only the top-ranked product for each month.

Window functions provide advanced analytical capabilities in SQL that allow you to rank, analyze, and compare data in a way that would be difficult with traditional SQL queries. Functions like ROW_NUMBER(), RANK(), LEAD(), and LAG() allow you to perform complex data analysis tasks such as ranking, cumulative calculations, and comparing values across rows.

These functions are essential tools for **time-series analysis**, **trend detection**, and **comparative analysis**, and they are widely used in industries such as finance, marketing, and sales. Understanding how to use window functions will significantly enhance your ability to work with large, complex datasets.

In the next chapter, we will explore **Common Table Expressions (CTEs)** and how they can be used to simplify complex queries, improve readability, and manage subqueries effectively.

Chapter 10: Working with Dates and Times

DATE Functions: DATEADD, DATEDIFF, EXTRACT, and More

Dates and times are fundamental elements in many data analysis tasks, especially when dealing with time-series data, event logs, or any analysis based on dates. SQL provides several functions to manipulate, extract, and compare date and time values.

Let's dive into some of the most commonly used **date functions** in SQL:

---

1. DATEADD: Adding or Subtracting Time Intervals

The DATEADD() function allows you to add or subtract a specified time interval (such as days, months, or years) to a date or time. It's helpful for calculations like finding the date 30 days from today or subtracting a month from a date.

- **Syntax:**

```sql
Copy code
DATEADD(interval, number, date)
```

- o interval: The part of the date to add (e.g., DAY, MONTH, YEAR).
- o number: The number of intervals to add (can be positive or negative).
- o date: The date to which the interval is added.
- **Example**: Adding 10 days to a given date:

sql
Copy code
SELECT DATEADD(DAY, 10, '2024-01-01') AS new_date;
This will return 2024-01-11.

- **Example**: Subtracting 2 months from today:

sql
Copy code
SELECT   DATEADD(MONTH,   -2,   GETDATE())   AS
two_months_ago;
This will return the date that is 2 months prior to today.

---

2. DATEDIFF: Calculating the Difference Between Two Dates

The DATEDIFF() function calculates the difference between two dates and returns the result as an integer representing the number of specified units (e.g., days, months, years) between the dates.

- **Syntax**:

sql

Copy code

DATEDIFF(interval, date1, date2)

- o interval: The unit of time to measure (e.g., DAY, MONTH, YEAR).
- o date1 and date2: The two dates to compare.
- **Example**: Finding the number of days between two dates:

sql

Copy code

SELECT DATEDIFF(DAY, '2024-01-01', '2024-02-01') AS date_diff;

This will return 31, as there are 31 days between January 1, 2024, and February 1, 2024.

- **Example**: Finding the number of years between a birthdate and today's date:

sql

Copy code

SELECT DATEDIFF(YEAR, '1990-05-10', GETDATE()) AS age;

This will return the age of someone born on May 10, 1990.

---

3. EXTRACT: Extracting Parts of a Date or Time

The EXTRACT() function is used to retrieve specific parts of a date or time (e.g., year, month, day, weekday, etc.). This is useful when you need to analyze or group data based on specific date components.

- **Syntax**:

sql
Copy code
EXTRACT(part FROM date)

  - o   part: The part of the date or time to extract (e.g., YEAR, MONTH, DAY, WEEKDAY).
  - o   date: The date or time from which to extract the part.
- **Example**: Extracting the year and month from a date:

sql
Copy code
SELECT EXTRACT(YEAR FROM '2024-01-01') AS year,
      EXTRACT(MONTH FROM '2024-01-01') AS month;
This will return:

  - o   year: 2024
  - o   month: 1
- **Example**: Extracting the day of the week:

sql
Copy code
SELECT EXTRACT(DOW FROM '2024-01-01') AS weekday;
This will return the day of the week as an integer (0 for Sunday, 1 for Monday, and so on).

4. GETDATE() and CURRENT_TIMESTAMP: Getting the Current Date and Time

The GETDATE() function (or CURRENT_TIMESTAMP in some SQL variants) returns the current date and time of the system.

- **Example**:

  sql
  Copy code
  SELECT GETDATE() AS current_date_time;

  This will return the current date and time at the moment the query is executed.

Time Zones and Format Issues

When working with dates and times, particularly when data comes from multiple time zones or needs to be presented in different formats, understanding how to handle time zones and formats is crucial.

1. Handling Time Zones

Many databases, including PostgreSQL and MySQL, support **time zone management**. If you're working with global data, you may need to store dates in UTC (Coordinated Universal Time) and convert them to local time zones for analysis or reporting.

- **Converting UTC to Local Time**: In PostgreSQL, the AT TIME ZONE clause can be used to convert times from one time zone to another.

  - **Example**: Converting UTC to a specific time zone:

    sql
    Copy code
    ```sql
    SELECT '2024-01-01 12:00:00'::timestamp AT TIME ZONE 'UTC' AT TIME ZONE 'America/New_York';
    ```

    This converts a timestamp from UTC to the Eastern Time Zone (New York).

- **Time Zone Conversion in MySQL**: MySQL has built-in support for time zones, but you need to ensure that your server is configured to use them correctly. You can use the CONVERT_TZ() function to convert between time zones.

  - **Example**: Converting UTC to a specific time zone:

    sql
    Copy code
    ```sql
    SELECT CONVERT_TZ('2024-01-01 12:00:00', '+00:00', '-05:00');
    ```

    This converts a timestamp from UTC (+00:00) to Eastern Standard Time (-05:00).

2. Formatting Dates and Times

Different systems and use cases may require specific date formats, so it's important to know how to **format** dates and times.

- **MySQL**: Use DATE_FORMAT() to format dates.
    - **Example**: Formatting a date as YYYY-MM-DD:

      sql
      Copy code
      ```sql
      SELECT DATE_FORMAT('2024-01-01', '%Y-%m-%d') AS formatted_date;
      ```

      This will return 2024-01-01.

- **PostgreSQL**: Use the TO_CHAR() function to format dates.
    - **Example**: Formatting a date as MM/DD/YYYY:

      sql
      Copy code
      ```sql
      SELECT TO_CHAR('2024-01-01'::date, 'MM/DD/YYYY') AS formatted_date;
      ```

      This will return 01/01/2024.

Real-World Example: Analyzing Seasonal Trends in Website Traffic

Suppose you are analyzing website traffic data for an e-commerce platform. You want to determine how website traffic varies by season—specifically, you want to know if traffic increases during the holiday season (November and December).

The **traffic data** is stored in a table with the following columns:

- visitor_id: Unique identifier for each visitor
- visit_date: Date of the visit
- page_views: Number of pages viewed during the visit

To identify seasonal traffic trends, you need to extract the month from the visit_date and aggregate the number of page views by month to compare the results.

Step 1: Extract Month and Year from the Visit Date

sql

Copy code

```
SELECT EXTRACT(YEAR FROM visit_date) AS year,
    EXTRACT(MONTH FROM visit_date) AS month,
    SUM(page_views) AS total_page_views
FROM website_traffic
GROUP BY year, month
ORDER BY year, month;
```

This query will return the total number of page views for each month, allowing you to identify trends across the entire year.

Step 2: Analyzing Seasonal Trends

To specifically focus on the holiday months (November and December), you can filter for these months and analyze the results.

```sql
Copy code
SELECT EXTRACT(YEAR FROM visit_date) AS year,
    EXTRACT(MONTH FROM visit_date) AS month,
    SUM(page_views) AS total_page_views
FROM website_traffic
WHERE EXTRACT(MONTH FROM visit_date) IN (11, 12)
GROUP BY year, month
ORDER BY year, month;
```

This will show you the page views during the holiday months across different years. You can compare these months to others (such as January and February) to determine if there is a seasonal spike in traffic.

Working with dates and times in SQL is essential for many data science tasks, particularly when analyzing time-series data, seasonal trends, or any event-based data. SQL provides a variety of functions like DATEADD(), DATEDIFF(), and EXTRACT() to manipulate and extract meaningful insights from date and time fields.

By understanding how to handle time zones, format dates, and calculate intervals, you can ensure accurate and effective analysis of time-related data. As shown in the real-world example, working with seasonal trends is a typical application of these functions, and mastering date and time manipulation can enhance your analytical capabilities in data science.

In the next chapter, we will dive into **Common Table Expressions (CTEs)**, which allow you to write more modular, readable, and reusable SQL queries.

Chapter 11: Indexing for Performance

What Are Indexes?

In the world of databases, **indexes** are like a book's table of contents—they allow for faster searching by providing a quick reference to data stored in a table, without having to scan every row. An **index** is a data structure that enhances the speed of retrieval operations on a database table at the cost of additional space and slower data modification operations like INSERT, UPDATE, or DELETE.

Indexes are used to efficiently look up data based on the values of one or more columns. By creating an index on a column, you can significantly improve the performance of queries that filter, sort, or join on that column.

How Indexes Speed Up Query Performance:

- **Faster Data Retrieval**: When you create an index on a column, the database engine doesn't need to scan the entire table for queries that filter on that column. Instead, it uses the index to quickly locate the matching rows.
- **Improved Sorting**: Indexes help with queries that include sorting (ORDER BY) because the data is already organized in a sorted order.

- **Faster Joins**: When you join tables on indexed columns, the join operation can be much faster because the database can quickly locate the matching rows in both tables using the indexes.

However, it's important to balance index creation with the performance cost on data modification operations. While queries will be faster, every time data is modified, the indexes need to be updated, which can slow down operations like inserts or updates.

Types of Indexes

There are various types of indexes in SQL, each optimized for different kinds of operations. Let's explore the most common types:

---

1. B-tree Index

A **B-tree index** is the most common type of index in SQL databases. It is a balanced tree structure where each node contains a range of values, and the leaves hold pointers to the actual data. B-tree indexes are particularly effective for queries that involve range searches (e.g., finding all records where a value is between two numbers) or equality searches.

- **Best for**: Range queries, equality comparisons, and queries with sorting (ORDER BY).

- **How it works**: B-tree indexes store values in a sorted order, allowing the database to perform binary search to find rows quickly. As the tree is balanced, it ensures efficient searching, even in large datasets.

- **Example**: If you have a table of employees with an employee_id column, a B-tree index on employee_id will make queries like:

sql
Copy code
SELECT * FROM employees WHERE employee_id = 123;
very fast, as the database can quickly find the correct row in the index.

---

2. Hash Index

A **hash index** uses a hash function to map column values to specific locations in the index. It is particularly fast for exact-match lookups but inefficient for range queries because the values are not stored in any particular order.

- **Best for**: Equality comparisons, such as when you use the = operator.

- **How it works**: The hash function converts the column value into a hash code, which is then used to locate the row in the index. Hash indexes are highly efficient for exact match searches but are not useful for queries that need to compare ranges (e.g., BETWEEN, >, <).

- **Example**: A hash index would be ideal for a query like:

sql
Copy code
SELECT * FROM employees WHERE employee_id = 123;
However, it would not be useful for queries like:

sql
Copy code
SELECT * FROM employees WHERE employee_id BETWEEN 100 AND 200;

---

3. Composite Index (Multi-column Index)

A **composite index** (also known as a multi-column index) is an index on two or more columns of a table. This type of index can significantly improve performance for queries that filter on multiple columns.

- **Best for**: Queries that filter or sort based on multiple columns.
- **How it works**: Composite indexes store a sorted list of column values in a multi-column order. For example, an index on the combination of first_name and last_name will improve the performance of queries like:

sql

Copy code
SELECT * FROM employees WHERE first_name = 'John' AND last_name = 'Doe';

- **Example**: You can create a composite index on multiple columns like:

sql
Copy code
CREATE INDEX idx_name ON employees (first_name, last_name);

This index will speed up any query that filters on both first_name and last_name, but it won't necessarily improve performance for queries that filter on only one of those columns.

---

4. Full-Text Index

A **full-text index** is used for full-text searching on text-based columns. It allows for fast text searches within large amounts of data, enabling functionality such as searching for keywords or phrases.

- **Best for**: Text searches, such as searching for specific words or phrases in large bodies of text.
- **How it works**: The database creates an index that stores information about the words in the text and their locations within the document. This allows for efficient searching without scanning the entire column.

- **Example**: In MySQL or PostgreSQL, you can create a full-text index on a column with a large amount of text data:

sql
Copy code

```
CREATE FULLTEXT INDEX idx_fulltext ON articles (content);
```

This allows you to perform a full-text search:

sql
Copy code

```
SELECT * FROM articles WHERE MATCH(content) AGAINST('database performance');
```

---

5. Unique Index

A **unique index** ensures that all values in a column (or a combination of columns) are distinct. This index is automatically created when you define a column as UNIQUE in your table schema. It can be useful for ensuring data integrity and preventing duplicate entries.

- **Best for**: Ensuring data uniqueness, such as when you want to enforce that email addresses or user IDs are unique in a table.
- **How it works**: When you insert or update data, the database checks the index to ensure that no duplicate values exist in the indexed column(s).

- **Example**: For a table of users, you might create a unique index on the email column:

sql

Copy code

CREATE UNIQUE INDEX idx_unique_email ON users (email);

This ensures that no two users can have the same email address in the database.

Real-World Example: Improving the Speed of Customer Searches in an E-Commerce Database

Imagine you're working on an e-commerce website with a large customer database. The website's performance is sluggish, especially when customers search for products or view their order histories. You've identified that searches are often performed on the customer_id, name, and email columns in the customers table.

To optimize these queries, you decide to add indexes to the relevant columns.

Step 1: Indexing the customer_id Column

Since customer_id is used frequently in search queries, adding an index on this column will speed up lookup times.

sql

Copy code

CREATE INDEX idx_customer_id ON customers (customer_id);

This index will speed up queries that filter by customer_id, such as:

sql

Copy code

```
SELECT * FROM customers WHERE customer_id = 123;
```

Step 2: Indexing the email Column for Fast Lookups

Customers often search for their accounts using their email addresses. You can add a unique index on the email column to both ensure data integrity and improve query speed.

sql

Copy code

```
CREATE UNIQUE INDEX idx_unique_email ON customers (email);
```

This ensures that each email address in the database is unique and also speeds up queries like:

sql

Copy code

```
SELECT * FROM customers WHERE email = 'customer@example.com';
```

Step 3: Composite Index for Name Search

If the application allows users to search for customers by first_name and last_name together, you can create a composite index to optimize those queries.

sql

Copy code

```
CREATE INDEX idx_name ON customers (first_name, last_name);
```

This index helps optimize queries such as:

sql

Copy code

```
SELECT * FROM customers WHERE first_name = 'John' AND last_name =
'Doe';
```

Indexes are crucial for improving the performance of SQL queries, especially when dealing with large datasets. By creating the appropriate indexes on frequently queried columns, you can significantly speed up data retrieval operations. However, it's important to keep in mind that while indexes speed up query performance, they can slow down data modification operations (like INSERT, UPDATE, and DELETE) because the indexes need to be updated whenever the underlying data changes.

In the next chapter, we will explore **Transactions and Concurrency Control**, which are key concepts for maintaining data integrity and ensuring that multiple users can access the database concurrently without conflicts.

Chapter 12: Transactions and Concurrency Control

ACID Properties: What Makes a Transaction Reliable

In the world of databases, **transactions** are sequences of operations that are treated as a single unit of work. A transaction guarantees that all operations within it are completed successfully before being permanently saved to the database. If anything goes wrong during the transaction, all changes can be rolled back to ensure data integrity. The **ACID properties** are the key to ensuring transactions are reliable, predictable, and maintainable.

ACID stands for:

- **Atomicity**: This property ensures that a transaction is treated as a single "atomic" unit of work. It means that either all operations in the transaction are executed successfully, or none of them are. If any operation within the transaction fails, the entire transaction is rolled back.

  Example: If you're transferring money from one bank account to another, either both the withdrawal from one account and the deposit into the other account happen, or neither happens. If one part of the transaction fails, the system ensures that neither account is modified.

- **Consistency**: A transaction takes the database from one consistent state to another. The database must remain in a valid state before and after the transaction. If a transaction violates any constraints, such as a unique constraint or foreign key constraint, the transaction will be rolled back.

Example: If you're adding a new product to an inventory system, the product must have a valid price and quantity, and it must adhere to any other business rules set in the database schema. The database will enforce these rules and prevent the transaction from committing if the data violates them.

- **Isolation**: Transactions are isolated from each other. The operations of one transaction should not interfere with the operations of another transaction. In other words, the intermediate state of a transaction is invisible to other transactions until the transaction is committed.

Example: If two users try to update the same product inventory simultaneously, their transactions should be handled in such a way that each one sees a consistent version of the data, and the final result is correct.

- **Durability**: Once a transaction is committed, its changes are permanent, even in the event of a system crash or failure. The database ensures that the committed data is stored securely and can be recovered after a failure.

  Example: After completing a bank transfer, the system ensures that the changes are permanent and will not be lost, even if the system crashes immediately after the transaction is committed.

Transaction Commands: COMMIT, ROLLBACK

To manage transactions in SQL, we use a few key commands that allow us to start, confirm, or undo transactions. These are essential for ensuring the integrity of the database when performing operations that involve multiple steps or are dependent on external conditions.

- **COMMIT**: The COMMIT command is used to save the changes made by a transaction to the database. When you issue a COMMIT, all the changes made within the transaction are permanently applied, and the transaction is considered complete.

  Example:

  sql

```
Copy code
BEGIN TRANSACTION;
UPDATE inventory SET stock = stock - 1 WHERE product_id = 101;
COMMIT;
```

This ensures that the inventory update for product 101 is saved and made permanent.

- **ROLLBACK**: The ROLLBACK command is used to undo all changes made in the current transaction. If an error occurs or if you decide not to proceed with the changes, ROLLBACK allows you to revert the database to its state before the transaction began.

Example:

```
sql
Copy code
BEGIN TRANSACTION;
UPDATE inventory SET stock = stock - 1 WHERE product_id = 101;
-- If an error occurs, rollback changes
ROLLBACK;
```

If something goes wrong during the transaction, such as a failure to update inventory due to a constraint violation, the ROLLBACK command ensures the inventory count is not reduced and the transaction does not leave the database in an inconsistent state.

- **SAVEPOINT**: Sometimes, you might want to create a point within a transaction that you can return to if needed. This is where SAVEPOINT comes in. It marks a point in a transaction to which you can later ROLLBACK without undoing the entire transaction.

Example:

```
sql
Copy code
BEGIN TRANSACTION;
SAVEPOINT step1;
UPDATE inventory SET stock = stock - 1 WHERE product_id = 101;
-- If something goes wrong later, roll back to step1
ROLLBACK TO step1;
COMMIT;
```

Real-World Example: Managing Inventory Updates in an E-Commerce System During High Traffic

Let's say you're managing an e-commerce system that handles inventory updates. During high traffic, multiple users may try to purchase the same product at the same time. In this case, transactions and concurrency control are crucial to ensuring that the inventory is correctly updated and that no overselling occurs.

Scenario:

Imagine an online store that sells a limited number of a specific product. Two customers, **Alice** and **Bob**, are trying to purchase the last item in stock at the same time.

- **Step 1: Transaction Starts for Alice**:
  - Alice initiates her purchase. The system starts a transaction to update the inventory, reducing the stock by one.
  - The system checks the inventory to see if the stock is available.
  - Since the item is in stock, the system proceeds to decrement the stock and records the transaction.
- **Step 2: Transaction Starts for Bob**:
  - Bob initiates his purchase simultaneously. The system starts a second transaction to check and update the inventory.
  - However, since Alice's transaction is still in progress, Bob's transaction might see the inventory as available, even though Alice has already reserved the last item.

To prevent this race condition, the system must use **isolation** to handle the concurrent transactions properly. There are different **isolation levels** in SQL that determine how transactions interact with each other:

- **Read Uncommitted**: Bob could potentially see uncommitted changes made by Alice, leading to a **dirty read**.

- **Read Committed**: Bob will only see committed changes. In this case, he might still be able to purchase the product before Alice's transaction is committed.

- **Repeatable Read**: This ensures that Bob can only read consistent data within the transaction. If Alice is updating the inventory, Bob will have to wait until Alice commits or rolls back her transaction.

- **Serializable**: This is the strictest isolation level. It guarantees that transactions are executed one after the other, preventing any conflicting operations.

In this scenario, we might use a **serializable isolation level** to ensure that Alice's and Bob's transactions do not conflict. If Alice successfully purchases the last product, Bob's transaction will be rolled back, and he will receive a notification that the item is out of stock.

SQL Code Example: Managing Inventory Transactions

```
sql
Copy code
BEGIN TRANSACTION;

-- Alice attempts to purchase a product
```

```
UPDATE inventory SET stock = stock - 1 WHERE product_id = 101 AND
stock > 0;
IF (ROW_COUNT() = 0) THEN
  -- If no rows were affected, the stock was insufficient
  ROLLBACK;
  -- Return 'out of stock' message
  RETURN;
END IF;


-- Finalize the transaction after successful update
COMMIT;
```

In this example:

- We begin a transaction and try to update the inventory.
- The WHERE clause ensures that the stock is only updated if there's stock available.
- If no rows are affected (i.e., no products were available), we ROLLBACK the transaction.
- If the inventory update is successful, we COMMIT the transaction, making the change permanent.

Transactions and concurrency control are vital aspects of database management, especially in environments with high traffic or critical data. The **ACID properties** ensure that transactions are reliable, maintaining data integrity and consistency even in the face of system failures or concurrent operations. By using transaction commands like COMMIT, ROLLBACK, and SAVEPOINT, you can better manage database changes, prevent data corruption, and improve performance.

In the next chapter, we will delve into **Database Normalization**, exploring how to organize data efficiently to reduce redundancy and ensure integrity in large datasets.

Chapter 13: Normalization and Database Design

What is Database Normalization?

Database normalization is the process of organizing a relational database in such a way that it reduces redundancy and dependency, ensuring that the data is stored efficiently and without unnecessary repetition. Normalization aims to separate data into related tables and eliminate duplicate data, which in turn helps improve the structure of the database, simplifies maintenance, and reduces the risk of anomalies during updates, deletions, or insertions.

The main goal of normalization is to ensure that the database adheres to certain rules (called **normal forms**) that optimize the data structure. By applying normalization, we can avoid issues like data inconsistency, update anomalies, and deletion anomalies.

Normal Forms: 1NF, 2NF, 3NF, etc.

There are several stages of normalization, called **normal forms (NF)**. Each normal form builds on the previous one, aiming to eliminate specific types of redundancy and dependency. The most commonly used normal forms are **1NF**, **2NF**, and **3NF**. Let's break them down:

1NF: First Normal Form

A table is in **First Normal Form (1NF)** if:

- All columns contain **atomic values** (i.e., indivisible values).
- Each column contains values of a **single type** (no lists or sets of values).
- Each row is unique and has a **primary key**.

The main goal of 1NF is to ensure that the data is in a flat structure, with no repeating groups or arrays within a column.

Example: Suppose you have a table that stores customer orders, and one of the columns contains a list of items ordered:

Customer ID	Customer Name	Ordered Items
1	Alice	Apple, Banana
2	Bob	Banana, Orange, Apple

This violates 1NF because the "Ordered Items" column contains multiple values (a list) for a single row. To bring this into 1NF, we would separate the items into individual rows.

Customer ID	Customer Name	Ordered Item
1	Alice	Apple
1	Alice	Banana

Customer ID Customer Name Ordered Item

Customer ID	Customer Name	Ordered Item
2	Bob	Banana
2	Bob	Orange
2	Bob	Apple

Now, each row contains a single atomic value for "Ordered Item," which adheres to 1NF.

2NF: Second Normal Form

A table is in **Second Normal Form (2NF)** if:

- It is in **1NF**.
- It has **no partial dependency**, meaning that non-key columns depend on the entire primary key, not just part of it.

Partial dependency occurs when a non-key column is dependent on only a part of the primary key, rather than the whole key. This typically happens when the primary key is a **composite key** (i.e., made up of more than one column).

Example: Consider a table storing information about student courses, where the primary key is a combination of **Student ID** and **Course ID**:

Student ID	Course ID	Instructor	Instructor Email
1	101	Dr. Smith	smith@school.com
1	102	Dr. Johnson	johnson@school.com
2	101	Dr. Smith	smith@school.com

Here, the **Instructor** and **Instructor Email** columns are dependent only on the **Course ID** and not on the entire composite key (**Student ID, Course ID**). This is a partial dependency, which violates 2NF.

To bring this into 2NF, we would split the data into two tables: one for the student-course relationship, and another for the course-instructor relationship.

Student-Course Table:

Student ID	Course ID
1	101
1	102
2	101

Course Table:

Course ID	Instructor	Instructor Email

Course ID Instructor   Instructor Email

Course ID	Instructor	Instructor Email
101	Dr. Smith	smith@school.com
102	Dr. Johnson	johnson@school.com

Now, each non-key column (Instructor, Instructor Email) depends on the full primary key in the relevant table, satisfying 2NF.

3NF: Third Normal Form

A table is in **Third Normal Form (3NF)** if:

- It is in **2NF**.
- It has **no transitive dependency**, meaning that non-key columns are not dependent on other non-key columns.

Transitive dependency occurs when one non-key column depends on another non-key column, which then depends on the primary key.

Example: Suppose we have the following table:

Student ID Course ID Instructor   Instructor Office

Student ID	Course ID	Instructor	Instructor Office
1	101	Dr. Smith	Room 101
2	102	Dr. Johnson	Room 102

In this case, the **Instructor Office** column depends on **Instructor**, not on the primary key (**Student ID, Course ID**). This is a transitive dependency. To normalize this to 3NF, we would split the table into two:

Student-Course Table:

Student ID	Course ID	Instructor
1	101	Dr. Smith
2	102	Dr. Johnson

Instructor Table:

Instructor	Instructor Office
Dr. Smith	Room 101
Dr. Johnson	Room 102

Now, there are no transitive dependencies, and the table structure adheres to 3NF.

Higher Normal Forms (BCNF, 4NF, 5NF, etc.)

While **3NF** is sufficient for most use cases, there are higher normal forms such as **Boyce-Codd Normal Form (BCNF)**, **4NF**, and **5NF**, which address more specific types of redundancy and anomalies. For example:

- **BCNF** deals with situations where a table is in 3NF but still has certain kinds of redundancy.

- **4NF** addresses multi-valued dependencies, and **5NF** addresses cases where a table can be decomposed into smaller tables without losing information.

For the purpose of this book, we will focus primarily on **1NF**, **2NF**, and **3NF**, which are the most commonly used in real-world database design.

Real-World Example: Designing a Database for a School Management System

To illustrate the importance of normalization, let's consider designing a database for a **school management system**. The system must store information about students, courses, instructors, and enrollments. We will go through the steps of normalization to ensure that the database design is efficient and avoids redundancy.

Unnormalized Table (0NF):

Student ID	Student Name	Course ID	Course Name	Instructor	Instructor Email
1	Alice	101	Math	Dr. Smith	smith@school.com
1	Alice	102	English	Dr. Johnson	johnson@school.com

Student ID	Student Name	Course ID	Course Name	Instructor	Instructor Email
2	Bob	101	Math	Dr. Smith	smith@school.com

This table violates several normalization rules, including repeating course and instructor data for each student.

Step 1: First Normal Form (1NF)

- Separate multiple values in columns into individual rows.
- Remove repeating groups.

Student ID	Student Name	Course ID	Course Name	Instructor	Instructor Email
1	Alice	101	Math	Dr. Smith	smith@school.com
1	Alice	102	English	Dr. Johnson	johnson@school.com
2	Bob	101	Math	Dr. Smith	smith@school.com

Step 2: Second Normal Form (2NF)

- Remove partial dependencies by creating separate tables for students and courses.

Student-Course Table:

Student ID Course ID

Student ID	Course ID
1	101
1	102
2	101

Course Table:

Course ID	Course Name	Instructor	Instructor Email
101	Math	Dr. Smith	smith@school.com
102	English	Dr. Johnson	johnson@school.com

Step 3: Third Normal Form (3NF)

- Remove transitive dependencies by creating a separate table for instructors.

Instructor Table:

Instructor	Instructor Email
Dr. Smith	smith@school.com
Dr. Johnson	johnson@school.com

Now the database is properly normalized, with minimal redundancy and optimal structure for future queries and maintenance.

Normalization is an essential process for designing efficient and reliable databases. By following the rules of **1NF**, **2NF**, and **3NF**, we ensure that data is organized in a way that minimizes redundancy and dependency, leading to better performance, easier maintenance, and fewer data anomalies.

In the next chapter, we will explore **Database Relationships and Keys**, examining how to establish proper connections between different tables using primary, foreign, and composite keys.

Chapter 14: Data Modeling and Entity-Relationship Diagrams (ERD)

What is Data Modeling?

Data modeling is the process of creating a visual representation of a database structure. It defines how data is organized, how different data elements relate to each other, and how they will be stored in a database system. The goal of data modeling is to ensure that the database will support business needs efficiently, minimizing redundancy and maximizing data integrity.

There are several types of data models, ranging from conceptual models (high-level) to logical and physical models (detailed implementation). The most common type of diagram used for data modeling is the **Entity-Relationship Diagram (ERD)**, which helps visualize the relationships between different entities (tables) in a database.

Creating ERDs: Relationships Between Entities (Tables)

An **Entity-Relationship Diagram (ERD)** is a graphical representation of entities and their relationships to each other within a system. Entities usually correspond to database tables, and relationships describe how these tables are linked. In an ERD, the entities are represented as rectangles, while the relationships are shown as diamonds or lines connecting the entities.

There are three main types of relationships in an ERD:

1. **One-to-One (1:1)**: Each record in one table is related to only one record in another table.

2. **One-to-Many (1:N)**: A record in one table can relate to multiple records in another table.

3. **Many-to-Many (M:N)**: Multiple records in one table can relate to multiple records in another table.

An ERD also includes **attributes** (columns), which are represented by ovals attached to their respective entities. Attributes can be simple (atomic), composite, or multi-valued. Additionally, **primary keys (PK)** and **foreign keys (FK)** are often included in the ERD to denote relationships and constraints.

Basic Components of an ERD:

- **Entities**: These are typically represented by rectangles. In the context of relational databases, entities often translate to tables.

- **Attributes**: These are details about entities. In a database, attributes are columns in the table.

- **Primary Key (PK)**: A unique identifier for each record in an entity.

- **Foreign Key (FK)**: A reference to a primary key in another entity, establishing a relationship between tables.
- **Relationships**: These describe how entities are related to one another. Lines or diamonds represent relationships between tables.

ERD Symbols:

- **Rectangle**: Represents an entity (a table in the database).
- **Oval**: Represents an attribute of the entity.
- **Diamond**: Represents a relationship between entities.
- **Line**: Connects entities and relationships.
- **Double Ovals**: Represent multi-valued attributes.

Types of ERD Relationships:

1. **One-to-One (1:1)**: In a one-to-one relationship, one record in the first table is related to one record in the second table. For example, in a **Customer** and **Customer Profile** table, each customer has one unique profile.

   Example:

   o **Customer Table**: Stores customer details.
   o **Customer Profile Table**: Stores additional personal information (e.g., date of birth, preferences).

ERD Representation:

- o The **Customer** table and **Customer Profile** table are connected by a single line indicating that each customer has only one profile.

2. **One-to-Many (1:N)**: A one-to-many relationship occurs when one record in a table can be associated with multiple records in another table. This is one of the most common relationships in relational databases.

Example:

- o **Author Table**: Stores author details.
- o **Book Table**: Stores details of books written by authors.

ERD Representation:

- o A one-to-many relationship is represented with a line from the **Author** table to the **Book** table, with a crow's foot (symbolizing "many") on the **Book** side, indicating that one author can write multiple books.

3. **Many-to-Many (M:N)**: In a many-to-many relationship, multiple records in one table are associated with multiple records in another table. This requires an intermediate table, often referred to as a **junction table**, to resolve the relationship.

Example:

- o **Student Table**: Stores student details.
- o **Course Table**: Stores courses offered by the institution.
- o **Enrollment Table**: Resolves the many-to-many relationship by linking students to the courses they are enrolled in.

ERD Representation:

- o The **Student** and **Course** tables are connected by the **Enrollment** table. The **Enrollment** table has foreign keys referencing both the **Student** and **Course** tables.

Real-World Example: Modeling a Database for an Online Library System

To understand how data modeling and ERDs work in practice, let's design a simple database for an **online library system**. In this system, we will store information about **books, authors, members** (who borrow books), and **transactions** (book borrowings).

Step 1: Identify Entities

In the case of the library system, we identify the following entities:

- **Book**: Stores information about each book.
- **Author**: Stores information about each author.
- **Member**: Stores information about library members.
- **Transaction**: Stores borrowing records, tracking which member borrowed which book and when.

Step 2: Define Attributes

Each entity will have relevant attributes (columns) associated with it:

- **Book**: Book ID (PK), Title, Genre, Publish Year, Author ID (FK).
- **Author**: Author ID (PK), Name, Date of Birth.
- **Member**: Member ID (PK), Name, Email, Membership Date.
- **Transaction**: Transaction ID (PK), Book ID (FK), Member ID (FK), Borrow Date, Return Date.

Step 3: Define Relationships

- **Book - Author**: A **one-to-many** relationship. Each book is written by one author, but an author can write multiple books.
- **Member - Transaction**: A **one-to-many** relationship. Each member can borrow many books, but each transaction is associated with only one member.

- **Book - Transaction**: A **one-to-many** relationship. A book can be borrowed multiple times, but each transaction is linked to only one book.

Step 4: Create ERD

The ERD for the library system would look like this:

- The **Book** entity is connected to the **Author** entity by a one-to-many relationship. The **Book** table has a **Author ID (FK)** to reference the **Author** table.
- The **Member** entity is connected to the **Transaction** entity by a one-to-many relationship. The **Transaction** table contains a **Member ID (FK)**.
- The **Book** entity is also connected to the **Transaction** entity by a one-to-many relationship, with a **Book ID (FK)** in the **Transaction** table.

ERD Diagram:

sql
Copy code

```
+--------------------+    +--------------------+    +--------------------+
|    Author    |<------|    Book    |<------|   Transaction   |
+--------------------+    +--------------------+    +--------------------+
| Author ID (PK)   |    | Book ID (PK)   |    | Transaction ID (PK)|
| Name         |    | Title      |    | Book ID (FK)    |
| Date of Birth    |    | Genre      |    | Member ID (FK)   |
+--------------------+    | Publish Year   |    | Borrow Date    |
```

133

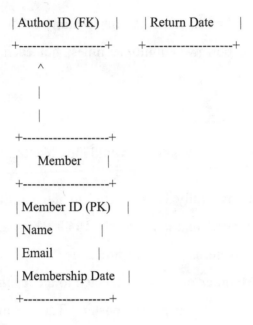

```
| Author ID (FK)   |        | Return Date    |
+-------------------+        +-------------------+
        ^
        |
        |
+-------------------+
|    Member    |
+-------------------+
| Member ID (PK)   |
| Name         |
| Email        |
| Membership Date   |
+-------------------+
```

In this ERD:

- The **Book** table references the **Author** table with the **Author ID** foreign key.
- The **Transaction** table references both the **Book** and **Member** tables using **Book ID** and **Member ID** foreign keys.

Data modeling and ERDs are essential tools for designing well-structured databases. By defining entities, their attributes, and the relationships between them, we can create a logical representation of how data will be stored and accessed. In the example of the online library system, the ERD provides a clear, visual representation of how books, authors, members, and transactions are connected.

In the next chapter, we will explore **Database Optimization and Query Tuning**, focusing on how to improve the performance of complex SQL queries, ensuring that the system runs efficiently even with large volumes of data.

Chapter 15: SQL for Data Science: Use Cases

SQL in Data Science: Key Use Cases

SQL is a foundational tool in the toolkit of a data scientist, enabling the retrieval, manipulation, and analysis of data stored in relational databases. Its widespread use across industries stems from its ability to efficiently manage large datasets, perform complex queries, and support a variety of data-driven tasks. Below are some of the key use cases of SQL in data science:

1. **Data Extraction**: One of the primary use cases for SQL is **data extraction**. SQL allows data scientists to extract specific subsets of data from large databases, such as filtering records based on certain conditions or aggregating data for analysis. For example, you might query a database to extract all customer transactions from a particular region or within a given date range.

   Example: Extracting a dataset of product sales for the past six months, filtered by sales region and product category.

   sql

   Copy code

   SELECT product_name, sales_amount, transaction_date

```
FROM sales
WHERE transaction_date BETWEEN '2024-01-01' AND '2024-06-30'
AND region = 'West'
AND product_category = 'Electronics';
```

2. **Data Cleaning**: Before analyzing data, it's often necessary to clean and preprocess it. SQL can handle various cleaning tasks, such as handling missing values, removing duplicates, and correcting data inconsistencies. For example, data scientists can use SQL to filter out null values or replace them with appropriate values.

   Example: Cleaning missing customer age data by setting a default value.

```sql
Copy code
UPDATE customers
SET age = 30
WHERE age IS NULL;
```

3. **Data Aggregation**: SQL is incredibly powerful when it comes to aggregating data. Data scientists frequently use aggregation functions like SUM(), AVG(), COUNT(), and GROUP BY to compute insights such as average sales, total revenue, or the number of unique customers.

   Example: Aggregating sales data by region and product category.

```
sql
Copy code
SELECT region, product_category, SUM(sales_amount) AS total_sales
FROM sales
GROUP BY region, product_category;
```

4. **Reporting**: SQL is commonly used for generating reports, such as monthly or quarterly summaries, performance metrics, or KPI dashboards. Data scientists often prepare data using SQL before presenting it to stakeholders or integrating it into business intelligence tools.

   Example: Generating a quarterly sales report for an executive dashboard.

```
sql
Copy code
SELECT product_name, SUM(sales_amount) AS total_sales,
EXTRACT(QUARTER FROM transaction_date) AS quarter
FROM sales
WHERE transaction_date BETWEEN '2024-01-01' AND '2024-12-31'
GROUP BY product_name, EXTRACT(QUARTER FROM
transaction_date);
```

5. **Data Integration**: Data scientists often work with multiple data sources. SQL allows them to **join** data from various tables, databases, or even external sources. By using **JOINs**, data scientists can create unified datasets for analysis.

Example: Combining customer data with transaction history to identify purchasing patterns.

sql
Copy code
```
SELECT              customers.customer_id,              customers.name,
COUNT(transactions.transaction_id) AS total_purchases
FROM customers
LEFT   JOIN   transactions   ON   customers.customer_id   =
transactions.customer_id
GROUP BY customers.customer_id, customers.name;
```

6. **Preparing Data for Machine Learning**: SQL plays a crucial role in preparing datasets for machine learning. Data scientists can use SQL to select relevant features, filter records, and handle missing data. SQL also enables the creation of features directly within the database, reducing the need for data movement.

Example: Preparing data for a machine learning model by selecting features like age, income, and product purchase history.

sql
Copy code
```
SELECT customer_id, age, income, COUNT(product_id)  AS
products_bought
FROM customers
```

LEFT JOIN transactions ON customers.customer_id = transactions.customer_id

GROUP BY customer_id, age, income;

Once the data is ready, it can be exported to a data science environment (e.g., Python or R) for model training.

SQL vs. Other Tools: Comparing SQL with Python, R, etc.

While SQL is highly efficient for querying and manipulating relational data, it is often used in combination with other tools in data science. Below is a comparison of SQL with other popular data science tools like **Python** and **R**:

1. **SQL vs. Python**:
    o **SQL**: Ideal for querying and managing structured data within relational databases. It excels at data extraction, aggregation, and filtering directly from databases, which is important for working with large datasets.
    o **Python**: While Python can interact with SQL databases (using libraries like pandas, SQLAlchemy, and sqlite3), it is better suited for **data analysis**, **machine learning**, and **data visualization**. Python offers more flexibility for handling unstructured data, complex computations, and advanced statistical modeling.

- o **Use Case Comparison**: If you're working with a large dataset stored in a database and need to extract a subset for analysis, SQL is the best tool. If you need to build machine learning models or perform advanced statistical analysis, Python (with libraries like scikit-learn and pandas) is the better choice.

2. **SQL vs. R**:

- o **SQL**: Similar to Python, SQL is ideal for querying and managing relational data, particularly when the data is large and needs to be processed in the database before analysis.

- o **R**: R is a specialized tool for statistical analysis and data visualization. It excels in advanced statistical modeling, hypothesis testing, and producing publication-quality visualizations. R integrates well with SQL for data extraction but performs its core operations (like modeling and visualization) in a more specialized environment.

- o **Use Case Comparison**: SQL is the best tool for extracting and cleaning data from relational databases, while R is the better option for conducting statistical analyses and visualizing complex datasets.

3. **SQL vs. NoSQL**:

o **SQL**: SQL is used with relational databases that store structured data in tables with predefined schemas. It's great for structured data and ensures ACID (Atomicity, Consistency, Isolation, Durability) compliance, making it suitable for transactional systems.

o **NoSQL**: NoSQL databases (e.g., MongoDB, Cassandra) are designed for unstructured or semi-structured data and are more flexible in terms of schema design. These databases are often used when scalability, flexibility, and high write loads are more important than strict data consistency.

o **Use Case Comparison**: SQL is best suited for applications that require structured data and transactional consistency, while NoSQL is used for handling unstructured data, high-speed applications, or applications requiring flexible schema design.

Real-World Example: Using SQL to Prepare Data for Machine Learning Models

In machine learning, data preparation is a critical step that often involves filtering, cleaning, and aggregating raw data. SQL can be used to create a dataset that is ready for model training.

Scenario: We are building a machine learning model to predict customer churn (whether a customer will leave a service). The database contains information about customers, their subscription plans, their usage, and historical churn events.

Step 1: Data Extraction

We start by querying the database to extract the necessary data fields, such as customer demographics, subscription details, and churn status.

```sql
Copy code
SELECT customer_id, age, subscription_type, monthly_spend, churn_status, last_purchase_date
FROM customers
WHERE churn_status IS NOT NULL;
```

Step 2: Data Cleaning

We clean the data by handling missing values and outliers. For instance, we replace missing values for age with the average value.

```sql
Copy code
UPDATE customers
SET age = (SELECT AVG(age) FROM customers)
WHERE age IS NULL;
```

Step 3: Feature Engineering

We create new features that may be relevant for the machine learning model, such as the length of time a customer has been subscribed.

sql
Copy code
```sql
SELECT customer_id, DATEDIFF(CURDATE(), subscription_start_date) AS days_subscribed
FROM customers;
```

Step 4: Aggregation

Next, we aggregate customer behavior data, such as the number of purchases made in the last 30 days.

sql
Copy code
```sql
SELECT customer_id, COUNT(transaction_id) AS purchases_last_30_days
FROM transactions
WHERE transaction_date > CURDATE() - INTERVAL 30 DAY
GROUP BY customer_id;
```

Step 5: Combining Data

Finally, we combine all the prepared data into one dataset.

sql
Copy code
```sql
SELECT c.customer_id, c.age, c.subscription_type, c.monthly_spend, c.churn_status,
    f.purchases_last_30_days, DATEDIFF(CURDATE(), c.subscription_start_date) AS days_subscribed
FROM customers c
```

```
JOIN     (SELECT     customer_id,     COUNT(transaction_id)     AS
purchases_last_30_days
    FROM transactions
    WHERE transaction_date > CURDATE() - INTERVAL 30 DAY
    GROUP BY customer_id) f
ON c.customer_id = f.customer_id;
```

The resulting dataset can now be exported for use in training a machine learning model, such as a classification model to predict customer churn.

SQL plays a crucial role in data science, providing the foundation for efficient data extraction, cleaning, aggregation, and preparation for analysis and modeling. It complements other tools like Python and R, which excel in machine learning and statistical analysis. By mastering SQL, data scientists can efficiently handle large datasets, ensuring that the data is ready for more advanced analysis and predictive modeling.

In the next chapter, we will explore **Advanced SQL Techniques for Data Science**, covering topics such as window functions, subqueries, and optimization strategies for large datasets.

Chapter 16: Performance Tuning for Queries

Optimizing SQL Queries: How to Make Queries Run Faster

In the world of data science, performance matters—especially when working with large datasets. As data grows, queries that once ran quickly can start to slow down. This chapter covers techniques for **optimizing SQL queries** to ensure that they run efficiently and help data scientists work with large datasets without long wait times.

Here are key strategies to optimize your SQL queries:

1. **Use Indexes**: Indexes are one of the most effective ways to speed up query performance. By creating indexes on columns frequently used in WHERE clauses, JOIN conditions, and ORDER BY operations, SQL can quickly locate the necessary data without scanning the entire table.

   o **Example**: If you're often querying a product database based on the product name, creating an index on the product_name column will help speed up these queries.

   sql
   Copy code

CREATE INDEX idx_product_name ON products(product_name);

2. **Avoid SELECT * (Wildcard)**: Using SELECT * retrieves all columns from a table, which can be inefficient, especially when only a subset of the columns is needed. Specify only the columns you need to reduce the amount of data transferred.

   o **Example**: Instead of using SELECT *, select only the necessary columns.

   sql
   Copy code
   ```
   SELECT product_id, product_name, price
   FROM products
   WHERE product_category = 'Electronics';
   ```

3. **Use WHERE Clauses Effectively**: Filter data early in the query with WHERE clauses to limit the dataset. The smaller the dataset, the faster the query will run.

   o **Example**: If you're only interested in sales from a particular year, use a WHERE clause to filter out unnecessary data.

   sql
   Copy code
   ```
   SELECT product_name, SUM(sales_amount)
   FROM sales
   ```

WHERE YEAR(transaction_date) = 2024
GROUP BY product_name;

4. **Limit the Use of Subqueries**: Subqueries can be slower than joins, particularly if they are nested in SELECT, WHERE, or HAVING clauses. Instead of using subqueries, consider using JOINs, or in some cases, Common Table Expressions (CTEs) to improve readability and performance.

   o **Example**: Rather than using a subquery to find the highest sales per product, use a JOIN:

   ```sql
   Copy code
   SELECT     p.product_name,     SUM(s.sales_amount)     AS
   total_sales
   FROM products p
   JOIN sales s ON p.product_id = s.product_id
   GROUP BY p.product_name
   HAVING total_sales = (SELECT MAX(total_sales) FROM
   (SELECT SUM(sales_amount) AS total_sales FROM sales
   GROUP BY product_id) AS subquery);
   ```

5. **Avoid Redundant Calculations**: If you need to perform the same calculations multiple times, consider storing the result in a temporary table or a CTE. This reduces the need to recalculate the same values repeatedly.

   o **Example**: Storing intermediate results in a CTE for reuse in a query.

```
sql
Copy code
WITH sales_summary AS (
    SELECT product_id, SUM(sales_amount) AS total_sales
    FROM sales
    GROUP BY product_id
)
SELECT p.product_name, ss.total_sales
FROM products p
JOIN sales_summary ss ON p.product_id = ss.product_id;
```

6. **Limit Results with OFFSET and LIMIT**: For large datasets, especially in web applications, it's often useful to limit the number of results returned. Use LIMIT or TOP (depending on your SQL flavor) to restrict the number of rows retrieved, particularly in paginated queries.

   o **Example**: Fetching the top 10 products by sales:

```
sql
Copy code
SELECT product_name, SUM(sales_amount) AS total_sales
FROM sales
GROUP BY product_name
ORDER BY total_sales DESC
LIMIT 10;
```

EXPLAIN and Execution Plans: Understanding Query Performance

To truly understand how a query is being executed, we need to analyze its **execution plan**. The execution plan provides a step-by-step breakdown of how SQL processes a query, including details about indexes, joins, and data retrieval methods.

1. **EXPLAIN Keyword**: In most SQL databases (e.g., MySQL, PostgreSQL), the EXPLAIN keyword can be used before a query to show the execution plan. This helps identify bottlenecks, such as full table scans or inefficient joins.

   o **Example**: Use EXPLAIN to analyze a query's execution plan.

   sql
   Copy code
   ```
   EXPLAIN SELECT product_name, SUM(sales_amount)
   FROM sales
   WHERE YEAR(transaction_date) = 2024
   GROUP BY product_name;
   ```
   The output will include information on whether indexes are used, the type of join, and the estimated cost of each step in the query process.

2. **Interpreting the Execution Plan**: Key elements in an execution plan include:

   o **Table Scans**: If a table scan appears in the plan, it indicates that SQL is scanning the entire table. This is usually a sign that an index could improve performance.

o **Join Types**: INNER JOIN and LEFT JOIN are common. Inefficient joins can significantly slow down a query.

o **Index Usage**: If indexes are used, the query will likely perform faster.

o **Sorts and Aggregations**: Sorting large datasets or performing aggregations can be expensive operations. Consider optimizing these steps.

Real-World Example: Optimizing an E-commerce Product Search Query for Large Datasets

Imagine you're working on an e-commerce platform with millions of product records and you need to optimize the product search query. A typical search query might include filtering by product category, price range, and keyword matching in the product name.

Here's the initial query:

```sql
Copy code
SELECT product_name, price, description
FROM products
WHERE product_category = 'Electronics'
AND price BETWEEN 50 AND 500
```

AND product_name LIKE '%smartphone%';

Step 1: Analyzing the Execution Plan

We can start by examining the execution plan using EXPLAIN:

```sql
Copy code
EXPLAIN SELECT product_name, price, description
FROM products
WHERE product_category = 'Electronics'
AND price BETWEEN 50 AND 500
AND product_name LIKE '%smartphone%';
```

The execution plan might show that the query is performing a full table scan or using a slow LIKE operation, which can be inefficient, especially with wildcard matching at the beginning of a string (%smartphone).

Step 2: Adding Indexes

To speed up the query, we can add indexes on columns that are frequently filtered, such as product_category and price. Additionally, a **full-text index** could be useful for the product_name column.

```sql
Copy code
CREATE INDEX idx_product_category ON products(product_category);
CREATE INDEX idx_price ON products(price);
CREATE FULLTEXT INDEX idx_product_name ON products(product_name);
```

This indexing strategy improves performance by allowing SQL to quickly locate relevant rows based on the indexed columns.

Step 3: Refining the Query

Once indexes are in place, we can refine the query to ensure it makes the best use of those indexes. Avoid using LIKE '%term%', as it negates the benefits of an index. Instead, use full-text search capabilities or modify the query to reduce the need for wildcards at the start of the string.

If a full-text search index is created, the query would change to:

sql
Copy code

```
SELECT product_name, price, description
FROM products
WHERE product_category = 'Electronics'
AND price BETWEEN 50 AND 500
AND MATCH(product_name) AGAINST ('smartphone');
```

By using MATCH and AGAINST, the database will perform a more efficient full-text search.

Step 4: Using LIMIT for Pagination

For large datasets, it's often necessary to implement **pagination** so that the results can be broken into manageable chunks. You can add LIMIT and OFFSET to the query:

sql
Copy code

```
SELECT product_name, price, description
FROM products
WHERE product_category = 'Electronics'
```

AND price BETWEEN 50 AND 500

AND MATCH(product_name) AGAINST ('smartphone')

LIMIT 20 OFFSET 40;

This query retrieves 20 products, starting from the 41st result, for the next page in the search results.

Optimizing SQL queries is a crucial skill for any data scientist, especially when working with large datasets. By understanding and implementing performance tuning strategies—such as using indexes, avoiding wildcard queries, refining joins, and leveraging execution plans—you can significantly improve query performance. The right combination of techniques will ensure that data retrieval remains fast, even as the size of your data grows.

In the next chapter, we will dive into **Data Security in SQL**— exploring how to secure sensitive data, manage permissions, and protect against SQL injection attacks.

Chapter 17: Data Extraction and ETL

ETL Process: Extract, Transform, Load with SQL

The **ETL process** (Extract, Transform, Load) is a critical component of data management in data science and business intelligence. It involves extracting data from multiple sources, transforming it into a usable format, and then loading it into a target database or data warehouse for analysis. SQL plays a significant role in each of these steps, making it easier to clean, manipulate, and integrate data efficiently.

Let's break down the key stages of the ETL process:

1. **Extract**: In this phase, data is gathered from various sources, which could be databases, flat files, APIs, or other data systems. SQL is commonly used to query databases to extract the necessary data.

   o **Example**: Suppose you want to extract customer data from a transactional database to perform analysis. You might use a SELECT query to pull relevant data such as customer IDs, names, and contact information.

      sql
      Copy code

```
SELECT customer_id, customer_name, contact_info
FROM customers
WHERE account_status = 'Active';
```

2. **Transform**: During the transformation step, the extracted data is cleaned, formatted, and structured into a form suitable for analysis. SQL is powerful for performing transformations like filtering, merging datasets, applying business rules, and aggregating data.

    o   **Example**: After extracting data, you may need to clean it by transforming date formats, handling missing values, and categorizing data based on certain criteria.

    sql
    Copy code
    ```
    UPDATE customer_data
    SET registration_date = STR_TO_DATE(registration_date, '%d/%m/%Y')
    WHERE registration_date IS NOT NULL;
    ```
    Another common transformation could be categorizing age groups:

    sql
    Copy code
    ```
    CASE
      WHEN age BETWEEN 18 AND 24 THEN 'Young Adult'
      WHEN age BETWEEN 25 AND 40 THEN 'Adult'
      WHEN age BETWEEN 41 AND 60 THEN 'Mature Adult'
    ```

ELSE 'Senior'

END AS age_group

3. **Load**: The final phase involves loading the transformed data into a target database or data warehouse, making it available for further analysis. This could be done by using INSERT, UPDATE, or MERGE commands in SQL to load data into the target tables.

  o **Example**: After transforming the data, you can load it into an analytics database:

sql

Copy code

```
INSERT INTO customer_data_warehouse (customer_id, customer_name, age_group, registration_date)
SELECT customer_id, customer_name, age_group, registration_date
FROM transformed_customer_data;
```

Alternatively, you might use MERGE for loading data that needs to be updated or inserted based on matching keys.

sql

Copy code

```
MERGE INTO target_table AS target
USING source_table AS source
ON target.id = source.id
WHEN MATCHED THEN
  UPDATE SET target.value = source.value
```

WHEN NOT MATCHED THEN

INSERT (id, value) VALUES (source.id, source.value);

Using SQL for Data Pipelines: Connecting Databases with External Systems

In modern data science workflows, data often needs to be moved between various systems, databases, and external applications. SQL is commonly used to build **data pipelines** that automate the process of data extraction, transformation, and loading (ETL). Here's how SQL can be used within a data pipeline to integrate databases with external systems:

1. **Connecting to External Systems**: SQL can interact with external systems (such as APIs or other databases) through **connectors** or **integration tools**. Tools like Apache NiFi, Talend, or custom Python scripts often interface with databases using SQL queries to extract and load data.

   o **Example**: In an automated pipeline, you could set up a cron job that runs SQL queries on a scheduled basis to pull customer data from an external CRM system and load it into a centralized analytics database.

2. **Using APIs for Data Extraction**: Although SQL is not directly used to interact with APIs, it can be used within a larger pipeline, where SQL is responsible for querying

databases, while other tools (e.g., Python or Java) handle the extraction of data from external APIs.

- o **Example**: A Python script might call an API to retrieve customer information and then store the data in a relational database using SQL commands. The SQL commands can then handle the transformation (cleaning) and loading stages.

3. **Automation and Scheduling**: Once an ETL pipeline is in place, it is important to schedule data extraction and transformation tasks at regular intervals. SQL-based tools, along with job schedulers (like Apache Airflow), can be used to automate the process, reducing manual effort.

- o **Example**: A scheduled SQL job could run every night to extract and process the latest sales data, transform it into a suitable format for analysis, and load it into a reporting database for executives to access in the morning.

Real-World Example: Integrating Customer Data from Multiple Sources

Imagine a scenario where an e-commerce company needs to integrate customer data from multiple sources, including an internal CRM system, an external marketing tool, and a customer feedback survey database. The goal is to create a unified view of the customer to provide better insights for personalized marketing.

Here's how you might approach this with SQL in the ETL process:

1. **Extract**: Start by extracting customer data from the CRM system, marketing tool, and feedback survey database.

sql
Copy code

```
-- Extracting customer data from the CRM system
SELECT customer_id, first_name, last_name, email
FROM crm_customers
WHERE status = 'active';


-- Extracting marketing campaign data
SELECT customer_id, campaign_id, response
FROM marketing_campaigns
WHERE response_date >= '2024-01-01';


-- Extracting feedback survey data
SELECT customer_id, feedback_score, comments
FROM customer_feedback
WHERE feedback_date >= '2024-01-01';
```

2. **Transform**: Once data is extracted, transformations can be applied. For example, customer names might need to be standardized, feedback scores could be normalized, and data might need to be merged across the different sources.

sql

Copy code

```
-- Standardize customer names by combining first and last names
UPDATE crm_customers
SET full_name = CONCAT(first_name, ' ', last_name);

-- Normalize feedback scores (e.g., scale from 1-10)
UPDATE customer_feedback
SET feedback_score = CASE
  WHEN feedback_score > 5 THEN 'Positive'
  ELSE 'Negative'
END;
```

3. **Load**: Finally, the transformed data is loaded into a unified data warehouse, where it can be used for reporting, analysis, and insights.

sql

Copy code

```
INSERT INTO customer_data_warehouse (customer_id, full_name, email, feedback_score, campaign_response)
SELECT crm.customer_id, crm.full_name, crm.email, fb.feedback_score, mc.response
FROM crm_customers crm
LEFT JOIN customer_feedback fb ON crm.customer_id = fb.customer_id
LEFT JOIN marketing_campaigns mc ON crm.customer_id = mc.customer_id
WHERE crm.status = 'active';
```

Now, the data from multiple sources is integrated into a single table, making it easier to generate insights such as customer satisfaction scores, response rates to marketing campaigns, and more.

The **ETL process** is essential for preparing data for analysis and integrating data from multiple sources. SQL plays a critical role in each phase of the ETL pipeline by providing powerful tools for extracting, transforming, and loading data into databases. Understanding how to use SQL within data pipelines ensures that data can be seamlessly integrated, cleaned, and transformed for reporting and analysis.

In the next chapter, we will explore **Advanced SQL Techniques for Data Science** and discuss how to handle complex datasets, optimize performance, and work with distributed systems.

Chapter 18: Advanced Query Optimization

Indexing Strategies: How and When to Index

Indexes are one of the most powerful tools for optimizing SQL queries, particularly in large datasets. An index allows the database to quickly locate and access the data needed without having to scan the entire table. However, indexing is a trade-off—while it speeds up **SELECT** queries, it can slow down **INSERT, UPDATE,** and **DELETE** operations, as the indexes also need to be updated. The key is understanding **when** and **how** to index to maximize performance without introducing unnecessary overhead.

Key Concepts in Indexing:

1. **What is an Index?**
   An index in SQL is a data structure that improves the speed of data retrieval operations. It can be created on one or more columns and functions similarly to an index in a book, where it allows for quick lookup.

   o **Example**: In a sales database, you might create an index on the customer_id field to speed up queries that filter by customer.

   sql

Copy code
CREATE INDEX idx_customer_id ON sales (customer_id);

2. **When to Use Indexes:**

   o **Search Queries**: Indexes are particularly useful for columns frequently used in the **WHERE** clause, as they can drastically reduce query execution time.

   o **JOIN Operations**: Indexes on columns used in **JOIN** conditions can significantly reduce the time it takes to combine tables.

   o **Sorting and Filtering**: Columns often used with **ORDER BY**, **GROUP BY**, and **DISTINCT** can also benefit from indexes.

   o **Example**: If you're frequently searching for products by name, creating an index on the product_name column can speed up those queries.

   sql
   Copy code
   CREATE INDEX idx_product_name ON products (product_name);

3. **When to Avoid Indexes:**

   o **Write-heavy Tables**: If a table undergoes frequent **INSERT**, **UPDATE**, or **DELETE** operations, indexing can lead to performance degradation due to the need to update the index each time.

- o **Small Tables**: For small tables (typically fewer than a few thousand rows), indexing may not provide significant performance gains and might even reduce performance due to the overhead of maintaining the index.

4. **Types of Indexes:**

   - o **B-tree Indexes**: The default type of index, used for equality and range queries. It works well for most general-purpose indexing needs.

   - o **Hash Indexes**: Used for exact match queries. These are faster than B-tree indexes but do not support range queries.

   - o **Composite Indexes**: Indexes on multiple columns. Use composite indexes when queries frequently filter on multiple columns together.

     - **Example**: Indexing customer_id and order_date together if you often filter by both.

sql
Copy code
```
CREATE INDEX idx_customer_order ON sales (customer_id, order_date);
```

Query Refactoring: Writing Efficient Queries

Optimizing SQL queries through refactoring is a crucial skill for improving performance, especially when working with large datasets or complex joins. Query refactoring involves rewriting SQL queries to perform more efficiently, reducing the processing time and resource consumption.

Best Practices for Writing Efficient Queries:

1. **Select   Only   Necessary   Columns**: Instead of using SELECT * to retrieve all columns, specify only the columns needed for the result. This reduces the amount of data that needs to be processed.

   sql
   Copy code

   ```
   -- Less efficient
   SELECT * FROM orders;


   -- More efficient
   SELECT order_id, order_date, customer_id FROM orders;
   ```

2. **Use   WHERE   Clauses   to   Filter   Early**: Always apply filters as early as possible in your query to reduce the number of rows being processed. This is particularly important in **JOIN** and **GROUP BY** operations.

   sql
   Copy code

   ```
   -- Filter first
   SELECT customer_id, COUNT(*) FROM orders
   ```

WHERE order_date BETWEEN '2024-01-01' AND '2024-12-31'
GROUP BY customer_id;

3. **Avoid Using Subqueries in SELECT Clauses**: Subqueries in the **SELECT** clause can be slow because they are executed once for each row in the result set. Where possible, replace them with **JOINs** or **window functions**.

sql
Copy code
```
-- Avoid using subqueries in SELECT
SELECT customer_id,
    (SELECT COUNT(*) FROM orders WHERE orders.customer_id = customers.customer_id) AS order_count
FROM customers;


-- Use JOIN instead
SELECT customers.customer_id, COUNT(orders.order_id) AS order_count
FROM customers
LEFT JOIN orders ON customers.customer_id = orders.customer_id
GROUP BY customers.customer_id;
```

4. **Use Proper JOINs**: Always use the appropriate type of join. For example, use INNER JOIN for matching records, LEFT JOIN for including all rows from one table, and avoid using CROSS JOIN unless necessary (it can generate very large result sets).

sql

Copy code

-- Prefer INNER JOIN over CROSS JOIN

SELECT customers.customer_id, orders.order_id

FROM customers

INNER JOIN orders ON customers.customer_id = orders.customer_id;

5. **Avoid Functions in WHERE Clause**: Using functions like LOWER(), UPPER(), or SUBSTRING() in the **WHERE** clause prevents the database from using indexes efficiently. It's better to use such functions on the result set after the query is executed or to create an indexed computed column.

sql

Copy code

-- Inefficient

SELECT * FROM customers WHERE LOWER(customer_name) = 'john doe';

-- Efficient

SELECT * FROM customers WHERE customer_name = 'John Doe';

Real-World Example: Redesigning Complex Analytics Queries for a Large Sales Dataset

In large databases, running complex analytics queries can be resource-intensive and slow. Let's consider an example where a business wants to analyze sales data across multiple regions and products over time. The initial query might look like this:

sql
Copy code
```
SELECT region, product_name, SUM(sales_amount) AS total_sales,
AVG(sales_amount) AS avg_sales
FROM sales
WHERE sales_date BETWEEN '2024-01-01' AND '2024-12-31'
GROUP BY region, product_name
ORDER BY total_sales DESC;
```

While this query may work for smaller datasets, it can be inefficient for larger datasets due to several factors, including the number of rows and the time taken for sorting and grouping. To optimize it:

1. **Add Indexes**:
   Creating indexes on sales_date, region, and product_name will allow the database to quickly filter, group, and sort the data.

   sql
   Copy code
   ```
   CREATE INDEX idx_sales_date ON sales (sales_date);
   CREATE INDEX idx_region_product ON sales (region,
   product_name);
   ```

2. **Refactor the Query**:
   Instead of performing a full GROUP BY across all rows,

SQL FOR DATA SCIENCE

break the query into smaller steps, or use materialized views or temporary tables to pre-aggregate the data.

sql

Copy code

```
-- Using a materialized view for pre-aggregation
CREATE MATERIALIZED VIEW sales_summary AS
SELECT region, product_name, SUM(sales_amount) AS total_sales,
AVG(sales_amount) AS avg_sales
FROM sales
WHERE sales_date BETWEEN '2024-01-01' AND '2024-12-31'
GROUP BY region, product_name;

-- Querying the materialized view for final reporting
SELECT region, product_name, total_sales, avg_sales
FROM sales_summary
ORDER BY total_sales DESC;
```

3. **Optimize the JOINs:** If this query involves joining multiple tables (e.g., customers, products, etc.), ensure that the joins are done efficiently and that foreign keys are indexed.

sql

Copy code

```
SELECT region, product_name, SUM(s.sales_amount) AS total_sales
FROM sales s
JOIN products p ON s.product_id = p.product_id
JOIN regions r ON s.region_id = r.region_id
WHERE s.sales_date BETWEEN '2024-01-01' AND '2024-12-31'
```

GROUP BY region, product_name

ORDER BY total_sales DESC;

By breaking down complex queries, adding proper indexes, and avoiding unnecessary operations, the performance of analytics queries in large datasets can be dramatically improved.

Query optimization is an essential skill for anyone working with large datasets or complex SQL queries. By employing indexing strategies, refactoring inefficient queries, and understanding when and how to apply optimization techniques, you can significantly improve the performance of your SQL queries. In the next chapter, we'll delve into **Data Extraction and ETL** to explore how SQL can be used in building data pipelines and integrating various data sources.

Chapter 19: Handling Big Data with SQL

SQL in Big Data Environments: Using SQL with NoSQL and Distributed Systems

As the volume, velocity, and variety of data continue to grow, managing and processing large datasets becomes increasingly challenging. While traditional SQL databases (relational databases) are designed for structured data, the need for handling "big data" has led to the emergence of distributed systems and hybrid approaches that combine SQL with NoSQL technologies.

Big Data Overview:

1. **What is Big Data?**
   Big Data refers to datasets that are so large or complex that traditional data-processing software can't manage them effectively. These datasets often involve unstructured or semi-structured data and require specialized tools for storage, retrieval, and analysis.

   o **Examples** of Big Data include logs from web applications, sensor data from IoT devices, or vast amounts of social media posts.

2. **SQL and Big Data Integration**:
   SQL is traditionally used in relational databases, but with the advent of big data systems like **Hadoop**, **Spark**, and

NoSQL databases, SQL is now being integrated into big data environments.

- o **SQL-on-Hadoop**: Tools like **Apache Hive** and **Apache Impala** enable users to run SQL queries on Hadoop distributed file systems (HDFS), allowing data scientists and analysts to apply their SQL knowledge to process big data.

- o **SQL-on-NoSQL**: SQL-like query languages have been developed for NoSQL databases like **Cassandra, MongoDB**, and **Couchbase**, allowing users to interact with these databases using familiar SQL syntax or SQL-inspired commands.

- o **Example**: In a big data setup, you can use **Apache Hive** to run SQL queries on data stored in Hadoop's HDFS or use **Google BigQuery**, which runs SQL queries on large datasets in the cloud.

sql
Copy code
```sql
-- Running SQL on Hadoop using Hive
SELECT user_id, COUNT(*) AS page_views
FROM logs
WHERE timestamp BETWEEN '2024-01-01' AND '2024-12-31'
GROUP BY user_id;
```

3. **NoSQL Databases with SQL-Like Queries**:

- o **MongoDB**: MongoDB provides a SQL-like query language through its aggregation framework, allowing users to query data stored in a document-based format.

```js
Copy code
// Example of querying MongoDB with aggregation
db.logs.aggregate([
    { $match: { timestamp: { $gte: '2024-01-01', $lte: '2024-12-31' } } },
    { $group: { _id: "$user_id", page_views: { $sum: 1 } } }
]);
```

- o **Cassandra**: While Cassandra is a NoSQL database optimized for high availability and scalability, it provides a **CQL (Cassandra Query Language)** that closely resembles SQL for querying distributed data.

```cql
Copy code
-- Querying data in Cassandra using CQL
SELECT user_id, COUNT(*) FROM user_logs WHERE timestamp >= '2024-01-01' AND timestamp <= '2024-12-31' GROUP BY user_id;
```

Advantages of Using SQL in Big Data Environments:

- **Familiarity**: Data analysts and scientists can leverage their SQL knowledge when working with new big data tools.

- **Scalability**: SQL is now integrated into distributed systems that scale to handle petabytes of data.

- **Flexibility**: By using SQL-on-Hadoop or SQL-on-NoSQL, users can work with both structured and semi-structured data.

Data Warehousing Concepts: OLAP and OLTP

In big data environments, data warehousing plays a critical role in managing large datasets and supporting business intelligence. Understanding the differences between **OLAP (Online Analytical Processing)** and **OLTP (Online Transaction Processing)** systems is essential when designing or querying data warehouses.

1. OLAP (Online Analytical Processing):

- **Purpose**: OLAP systems are optimized for querying and analyzing large volumes of historical data. These systems are used primarily for **business intelligence (BI)** and **reporting**, enabling fast querying of aggregated data for trend analysis and decision-making.

- **Use Cases**: OLAP systems are widely used in applications like data mining, financial analysis, and business reporting, where complex queries and aggregations are needed.

- **Key Characteristics**:
  - o **Star Schema** or **Snowflake Schema**: Data is organized in multidimensional structures for easy querying and reporting.
  - o **Read-intensive**: OLAP systems are optimized for read-heavy workloads, where large datasets are aggregated and queried.
  - o **Batch Processing**: Data is processed in batches, and updates occur periodically (e.g., once a day or weekly).
- **Example**: A retailer might use OLAP to analyze sales data across regions, products, and time periods, allowing them to detect trends and make data-driven business decisions.

sql
Copy code
```sql
-- OLAP query example: Aggregating sales by region and product
SELECT region, product_category, SUM(sales_amount) AS total_sales
FROM sales_data
WHERE sales_date BETWEEN '2024-01-01' AND '2024-12-31'
GROUP BY region, product_category
ORDER BY total_sales DESC;
```

2. OLTP (Online Transaction Processing):

- **Purpose**: OLTP systems are designed for transactional applications that require fast and efficient data insertion, updating, and deletion. These systems are typically used in real-time applications such as e-commerce, banking, and customer relationship management (CRM).

- **Use Cases**: OLTP systems support applications that handle day-to-day operations, such as order processing, inventory management, and customer support.

- **Key Characteristics**:

  o **Normalized Data**: Data in OLTP systems is usually highly normalized to reduce redundancy and ensure data integrity.

  o **Write-intensive**: OLTP systems focus on fast transaction processing, handling a large volume of short, atomic transactions.

  o **Real-time Updates**: Changes to data are reflected immediately and in real time.

- **Example**: An online store uses OLTP systems to process customer orders, track inventory, and update the status of transactions in real time.

sql
Copy code

```sql
-- OLTP query example: Inserting a new customer order
INSERT INTO orders (customer_id, product_id, order_date, quantity, total_price)
VALUES (12345, 67890, '2024-12-04', 2, 49.98);
```

Real-World Example: Querying Massive Logs from a Web Application

Web applications generate large amounts of log data that need to be processed and analyzed for various reasons, such as tracking user behavior, identifying security issues, and troubleshooting performance problems. With Big Data tools and SQL, we can query and analyze this data efficiently.

Scenario: A web application generates log data every day, with each log entry recording information about user interactions (e.g., page views, errors, API requests). The logs are stored in a distributed system like Hadoop or a NoSQL database. We want to analyze the data to identify which pages have the most traffic in a given time period and determine if there are any performance bottlenecks.

1. **Using SQL with Hadoop (Apache Hive)**: Assume the logs are stored in a Hadoop cluster. We can use **Hive** to run SQL queries on this data, even though it's stored in the distributed filesystem.

```sql
Copy code
-- Querying web logs in Hive to find the most popular pages
SELECT page_url, COUNT(*) AS page_views
FROM web_logs
WHERE timestamp BETWEEN '2024-01-01' AND '2024-12-31'
GROUP BY page_url
```

ORDER BY page_views DESC;

2. **Using SQL with NoSQL (Cassandra)**: If the logs are stored in a NoSQL database like **Cassandra**, we can query the data using **CQL** (Cassandra Query Language), which is similar to SQL.

cql

Copy code

```
-- Querying web logs in Cassandra to count page views
SELECT page_url, COUNT(*) FROM web_logs
WHERE timestamp >= '2024-01-01' AND timestamp <= '2024-12-31'
GROUP BY page_url;
```

In this example, we are able to use SQL-like queries on large-scale log data to identify popular pages. SQL helps simplify the process of querying and analyzing big data in a way that is both familiar and efficient.

SQL's role in big data environments continues to grow as the need to manage and analyze vast amounts of data increases. By integrating SQL with distributed systems like Hadoop and NoSQL databases, as well as understanding key concepts like OLAP and OLTP, data professionals can leverage the power of SQL to handle big data challenges. In the next chapter, we will explore **Advanced**

Query Optimization to further enhance query performance in complex and large datasets.

Chapter 20: SQL in Cloud Platforms

SQL on Cloud Services: Using AWS RDS, Google Cloud SQL, Azure SQL

Cloud platforms have revolutionized the way we approach database management by providing scalable, reliable, and cost-effective services for hosting SQL databases. Major cloud providers like **Amazon Web Services (AWS)**, **Google Cloud**, and **Microsoft Azure** offer fully managed database services that allow you to run SQL databases without the complexities of manual database administration.

1. AWS RDS (Amazon Relational Database Service)

- **What   is   AWS   RDS?**
  Amazon RDS is a fully managed relational database service that supports multiple SQL database engines, including MySQL, PostgreSQL, MariaDB, Oracle, and SQL Server. With RDS, AWS handles routine database tasks such as backups, patch management, and scaling, allowing you to focus on your application's development.
- **Key Features**:
  - **Automated Backups**: RDS automatically creates backups and allows you to restore databases to any point in time within the retention period.

- o **Scaling**: You can scale your database instance vertically (by choosing more powerful instances) or horizontally (by using read replicas) to accommodate growing data or increased application demand.

- o **Security**: AWS provides encryption at rest and in transit, along with VPC integration for secure network access.

- **Example**:

A startup needs a reliable database for storing user profiles and transactional data for its web application. By using **AWS RDS with PostgreSQL**, the startup can deploy a fully managed database that scales with its needs without worrying about patching or manual backup management.

sql
Copy code

```
-- Sample query on AWS RDS (PostgreSQL) for user management
SELECT username, email, account_status
FROM users
WHERE account_status = 'active';
```

2. Google Cloud SQL

- **What is Google Cloud SQL?** Google Cloud SQL is a fully managed relational database service for MySQL, PostgreSQL, and SQL Server that runs on Google Cloud. It provides the benefits of cloud scalability, security, and ease of integration with other Google Cloud services.

- **Key Features**:
    - ○ **Automatic Backups and High Availability**: Cloud SQL offers automated backups and high-availability configurations, ensuring that your data is always protected and available.
    - ○ **Integration with Google Cloud Tools**: Cloud SQL easily integrates with other Google Cloud services like Google BigQuery, Cloud Pub/Sub, and Data Studio for analytics and reporting.
    - ○ **Scaling**: Similar to AWS, Google Cloud SQL allows both vertical and horizontal scaling.
- **Example**:

    A SaaS application uses **Google Cloud SQL with MySQL** to store customer subscription data. The application can scale its database as the user base grows while benefiting from the simplicity of Google Cloud's fully managed services.

sql
Copy code
```
-- Sample query on Google Cloud SQL (MySQL) for customer
subscriptions
SELECT customer_id, subscription_start_date, subscription_end_date
FROM subscriptions
WHERE subscription_end_date > CURDATE();
```

3. Microsoft Azure SQL Database

- **What is Azure SQL Database?**
  Azure SQL Database is a fully managed relational database service provided by Microsoft Azure, supporting SQL Server. It offers high performance, scalability, and robust security features for cloud-based applications.

- **Key Features**:
  - **Automatic Tuning**: Azure SQL Database uses machine learning to automatically optimize query performance and index management.
  - **High Availability and Disaster Recovery**: Azure offers built-in high availability through features like geo-replication and automatic failover.
  - **Flexible Pricing Models**: Azure provides different pricing tiers, such as Basic, Standard, and Premium, to cater to a variety of application needs.

- **Example**:
  A global e-commerce website utilizes **Azure SQL Database** to manage product inventory, customer orders, and order processing, ensuring smooth operation across multiple regions with low latency.

sql
Copy code
-- Sample query on Azure SQL Database for product inventory

```
SELECT product_id, product_name, stock_quantity
FROM products
WHERE stock_quantity > 0;
```

Benefits of Cloud Databases: Scalability, Cost-Effectiveness, and More

Cloud databases offer several benefits that make them a compelling choice for modern data-driven applications:

1. Scalability

- **Horizontal and Vertical Scaling**: Cloud databases allow both horizontal (adding more instances) and vertical (upgrading instance sizes) scaling. This ensures that the database can handle growing data volumes or increased user traffic without significant manual intervention.
- **Elasticity**: Many cloud platforms offer elastic scaling, meaning the database resources can automatically scale up or down based on traffic patterns or workload requirements, optimizing performance and costs.

Example: A media streaming service can automatically scale its database during peak viewing hours and scale it back down during off-peak hours, saving costs while ensuring high performance.

2. Cost-Effectiveness

- **Pay-as-you-go Pricing**: Cloud providers use a pay-as-you-go pricing model, which means you only pay for the database resources you use. This can be much more cost-effective than managing on-premise hardware.

- **Managed Services**: Cloud databases are fully managed, meaning you don't need to invest in hardware or allocate resources for routine database maintenance tasks like backups, security patching, and scaling.

Example: A small business can start with a basic database tier on a cloud platform and gradually scale as its user base grows, without having to worry about upfront infrastructure costs.

3. High Availability and Reliability

- **Built-in High Availability**: Cloud services provide multi-zone or multi-region replication to ensure your database is always available, even in the event of hardware failure or network issues.

- **Disaster Recovery**: Cloud databases provide automated backup solutions and can be restored to any point in time to recover from accidental deletions or system failures.

Example: A financial institution could store transaction data in a cloud database with high availability and disaster recovery, ensuring that its service is always operational and data is secure.

4. Security

- **Encryption**: Cloud databases typically come with built-in encryption mechanisms for data at rest and in transit, ensuring that sensitive data is protected.
- **Access Control**: Role-based access control (RBAC) allows businesses to control who has access to the database and what level of permissions they have.

Example: A healthcare company can use cloud databases to store patient data securely with access restricted to authorized medical professionals, ensuring compliance with regulations like HIPAA.

Real-World Example: Hosting a Cloud Database for a Startup's User Management System

A **startup** focusing on a SaaS product needs a scalable and reliable database solution to manage its growing user base. The company chooses to host its user management system on **AWS RDS with MySQL**.

Steps Taken:

1. **Database Selection**: The startup opts for MySQL on AWS RDS due to its familiarity, scalability, and compatibility with the application's requirements.

2. **Database Creation**: Using AWS's user-friendly interface, the startup creates an RDS instance with sufficient resources to handle its expected load.

3. **Data Security**: The company configures encryption for both data at rest and in transit, ensuring that user data is secure.

4. **Auto-Scaling Setup**: The RDS instance is set up to automatically scale vertically as traffic grows, and read replicas are used to distribute the read load.

5. **Backup and Recovery**: Automated backups are configured to ensure that the data can be restored if something goes wrong.

6. **Monitoring and Performance Tuning**: AWS CloudWatch is set up to monitor database performance, and auto-tuning options are enabled to optimize queries and indexing.

Outcome: The startup now has a cloud-based database solution that can scale with its growing user base while minimizing the overhead of managing infrastructure. The flexibility of AWS RDS also allows the startup to focus on developing its application rather than worrying about database maintenance.

Using SQL in cloud platforms such as **AWS RDS**, **Google Cloud SQL**, and **Azure SQL Database** provides startups and enterprises with powerful, cost-effective, and scalable database solutions. With the flexibility of cloud-based SQL databases, companies can easily scale their data storage and management solutions as their needs grow, without the complexities of traditional on-premise infrastructure. As we move forward in this book, we'll delve into more advanced SQL concepts, focusing on query optimization and advanced use cases that can further enhance data analysis and performance.

Chapter 21: SQL Security and Data Privacy

***

Securing Data with SQL: Encryption, Access Control, and More

In today's world, data security and privacy are top priorities for businesses and organizations that handle sensitive information. SQL databases, which store vast amounts of valuable data, must be properly secured to protect it from unauthorized access, breaches, and other potential threats. In this chapter, we will explore key security practices that help safeguard data in SQL databases, including encryption, access control, and more.

***

1. Encryption in SQL Databases

Encryption is the process of converting data into a format that is unreadable without a decryption key. It is one of the most fundamental techniques for securing sensitive data stored in SQL databases.

Types of Encryption:

- **Encryption at Rest**: This protects data stored on disk. Data at rest could include everything from tables to backups and transaction logs. Without proper encryption, if a database is compromised, attackers could steal data directly from disk.

Example:

- o In **AWS RDS** or **Azure SQL**, databases can be encrypted at rest using **AES (Advanced Encryption Standard)**. This ensures that the data stored in the database and its backups is unreadable without the proper keys.

sql
Copy code
```
-- Example: Enabling encryption in an Azure SQL Database
CREATE DATABASE MyDatabase
WITH ENCRYPTION;
```

- **Encryption in Transit**: This protects data during its movement from one system to another, ensuring that data is not exposed during transmission. This is especially important when SQL queries are being executed over networks.

Example:

- o SQL Server supports SSL encryption for encrypted connections between clients and databases. By enforcing SSL, you can ensure that the communication between your application and database remains secure.

```sql
Copy code
-- Example: Configuring encrypted SQL connection (MySQL)
-- Enable SSL for connections
-- Client Side:
mysql --ssl-ca=/path/to/ca-cert.pem --ssl-cert=/path/to/client-cert.pem --ssl-key=/path/to/client-key.pem -u user -p
```

- **Transparent Data Encryption (TDE)**: TDE automatically encrypts the data files and logs at the storage level, making it transparent to applications that interact with the database. SQL Server, Azure SQL, and other platforms support TDE.

Example:

  o In **SQL Server**, TDE can be enabled with the following command:

```sql
Copy code
-- Example: Enabling TDE in SQL Server
CREATE DATABASE MyDatabase
SET ENCRYPTION ON;
```

2. Access Control and User Management

Access control is one of the core components of database security. SQL databases allow the creation of roles and permissions that define who can access and modify data, ensuring that only authorized users can perform certain actions.

Role-Based Access Control (RBAC):

- **What is RBAC?**
  Role-based access control is a method of restricting access based on the roles assigned to users within an organization. Each role has a set of permissions that determine what actions the user can perform in the database.

  Example:

  o A healthcare database may have roles such as **Admin**, **Doctor**, and **Nurse**, with different levels of access. A doctor might be able to view patient data, while a nurse could only view certain sections like medical records, but not financial details.

sql
Copy code
```
-- Example: Creating a new role and assigning permissions
CREATE ROLE Doctor;
GRANT SELECT, UPDATE ON PatientRecords TO Doctor;
CREATE ROLE Nurse;
GRANT SELECT ON PatientRecords TO Nurse;
```

Least Privilege Principle:

- This principle dictates that users should only have the minimum level of access necessary to perform their job. By restricting access to only the essential parts of the database, you reduce the risk of unauthorized access or accidental data modifications.

  Example:

  - A nurse might only need access to read patient data, while a doctor needs both read and update access. A database administrator (DBA) would have full access to the database.

sql
Copy code
-- Example: Granting minimal privileges
GRANT SELECT ON PatientRecords TO Nurse;

Audit Trails:

- Monitoring and logging user activity can help identify potential security breaches and unauthorized access. Most SQL databases allow you to enable audit logging to track changes, logins, and other operations performed by users.

  Example:

- o In **MySQL**, you can enable the general log to track queries executed on the server:

sql
Copy code

```
-- Enabling query log in MySQL
SET global general_log = 1;
SET global log_output = 'table';
```

- o This helps maintain a trail of all user actions, useful for troubleshooting and detecting suspicious activity.

---

3. Data Privacy Regulations: GDPR, CCPA, and How SQL Can Help

With the increasing emphasis on data privacy, several regulations have been enacted to ensure that organizations handle user data responsibly and transparently. Two of the most widely discussed regulations are **GDPR (General Data Protection Regulation)** and **CCPA (California Consumer Privacy Act)**. These regulations impose strict rules on how personal data is stored, processed, and protected.

General Data Protection Regulation (GDPR):

- GDPR applies to any organization that collects or processes personal data of residents in the European Union. It mandates that organizations:

    o Obtain explicit consent before processing personal data.

    o Provide individuals with the right to access and delete their data.

    o Ensure the protection of data through encryption and other security measures.

SQL Considerations for GDPR:

    o SQL databases need to ensure that sensitive data such as names, email addresses, and other personal information is encrypted and can be easily queried for data access or deletion requests.

    o A **data retention policy** should be implemented to delete data after a certain period.

Example:

    ▪ When a user requests their data to be deleted (the "right to be forgotten"), SQL queries should be capable of identifying and removing all personally identifiable information (PII) from the database.

sql

Copy code

```
-- Example: Deleting personal data for GDPR compliance
DELETE FROM Users WHERE user_id = 12345;
```

California Consumer Privacy Act (CCPA):

- CCPA is a similar data privacy regulation focused on residents of California, USA. It gives consumers the right to:
  - Know what personal data is being collected about them.
  - Request deletion of their data.
  - Opt-out of the sale of their data.

SQL Considerations for CCPA:

  - SQL queries must be capable of identifying what data is being collected and where it's stored. Additionally, organizations must be able to comply with data access and deletion requests efficiently.

  ### Example:

    - A request for personal data under CCPA might look like this:

sql

Copy code

```
-- Example: Retrieving user information for CCPA request
SELECT * FROM Users WHERE email = 'user@example.com';
```

---

4. Real-World Example: Securing Sensitive Customer Data in a Healthcare Database

A healthcare organization stores sensitive patient information in its SQL database, including personal health records, diagnoses, and financial information. To ensure that this data is secure and complies with privacy regulations like **HIPAA** (Health Insurance Portability and Accountability Act), the organization implements various security measures:

1. **Encryption**:

   The healthcare database uses **AES-256 encryption** to encrypt all patient health records and financial information both at rest and in transit.

2. **Role-Based Access Control (RBAC)**:

   Different healthcare professionals have different levels of access. Doctors and medical staff can view sensitive health information, but only authorized personnel can access billing information.

sql

Copy code

```
-- Assigning different permissions based on roles
GRANT SELECT ON PatientHealthRecords TO Doctor;
```

GRANT SELECT, UPDATE ON PatientBilling TO Admin;

3. **Audit**   **Logging**:
   The organization enables audit logging to track who accessed patient records and when. This helps in maintaining an audit trail for compliance purposes.

```sql
Copy code
-- Enabling auditing in SQL Server
CREATE SERVER AUDIT MyAudit
    TO FILE (FILEPATH = 'C:\AuditLogs\');
```

4. **Compliance with GDPR and CCPA**:
   The healthcare organization ensures that users have the ability to request access to their data or request deletion, in compliance with GDPR and CCPA. When a patient requests their data to be deleted, the organization executes the following SQL query:

```sql
Copy code
-- Deleting patient data in response to a GDPR request
DELETE FROM PatientRecords WHERE patient_id = 101;
```

Securing data and maintaining privacy are paramount when working with SQL databases, especially when handling sensitive information. By employing encryption, access control, and adhering to data privacy regulations like **GDPR** and **CCPA**, organizations can mitigate the risk of data breaches and ensure compliance with international standards. The security practices discussed in this chapter help build a strong foundation for securing databases, protecting users' privacy, and meeting legal requirements. As the digital landscape evolves, it's essential to stay up to date with the latest security protocols and regulations to safeguard sensitive data effectively.

Chapter 22: Using SQL with Machine Learning

Integrating SQL with Machine Learning Models: Data Preparation and Extraction

SQL plays a crucial role in machine learning (ML), particularly when it comes to data preparation and extraction. ML models rely heavily on clean, well-structured, and relevant data to make accurate predictions. SQL is often the first step in this process, as it allows data scientists to efficiently query large datasets, filter out irrelevant information, and transform data into a format that can be fed into ML models.

---

1. Extracting Data for Machine Learning Models

Before any machine learning model can be trained, the first and most important step is to gather and prepare the data. SQL allows you to query relational databases to extract the necessary data for analysis.

- **Selecting Relevant Data**: SQL allows you to filter through large datasets and select only the data needed for a particular task. This includes filtering records, joining tables, and grouping data based on relevant attributes.

Example: In a customer churn prediction project, you would want to focus on data like customer demographics, account status, customer activity, and interaction history.

sql

Copy code

```
-- Example: Extracting customer data for churn prediction
SELECT customer_id, age, tenure, service_type, last_interaction,
is_churned
FROM customers
WHERE signup_date <= '2020-01-01';
```

In this query, you extract data such as customer ID, age, service type, and churn status, which will serve as input for the ML model.

- **Handling Time Series Data**: Machine learning models, particularly those dealing with forecasting or prediction over time, often require time-series data. SQL allows you to aggregate or extract time-series data efficiently by using functions such as DATE_TRUNC() or DATE_PART() in PostgreSQL or YEAR(), MONTH(), DAY() in MySQL.

Example: If you need customer interaction history over the last year, SQL can help you extract relevant features from the interaction logs.

sql

Copy code

```
-- Example: Aggregating customer interactions by month
```

```sql
SELECT    customer_id,    YEAR(interaction_date)    AS    year,
MONTH(interaction_date) AS month,
    COUNT(*) AS interaction_count
FROM customer_interactions
WHERE interaction_date BETWEEN '2023-01-01' AND '2023-12-31'
GROUP BY customer_id, year, month;
```

2. SQL for Feature Engineering: Transforming Data for Machine Learning

Feature engineering is one of the most critical steps in preparing data for machine learning. It involves creating new features or modifying existing ones to make the dataset more suitable for the model. SQL is extremely powerful for transforming raw data into features that are ready for machine learning.

- **Data Transformation and Feature Extraction**: Many machine learning models require numerical values, so data often needs to be transformed before it can be used. SQL can be used for these transformations—such as encoding categorical variables, normalizing data, or deriving new features from existing ones.

  Example: If you have customer age and tenure, you may want to create new features like "age group" or "customer lifetime value (CLV)".

  sql

Copy code

```
-- Example: Creating a new feature 'age_group' based on age ranges
SELECT customer_id,
    CASE
        WHEN age BETWEEN 18 AND 25 THEN '18-25'
        WHEN age BETWEEN 26 AND 35 THEN '26-35'
        WHEN age BETWEEN 36 AND 45 THEN '36-45'
        ELSE '46+'
    END AS age_group
FROM customers;
```

- **Normalizing Data**: Many machine learning algorithms, such as k-nearest neighbors or neural networks, perform better when the data is scaled. SQL can be used to normalize or standardize features.

Example: To normalize customer transaction data so that all features are on a similar scale, you might compute the min-max normalization for transaction amounts.

sql

Copy code

```
-- Example: Normalizing transaction amounts using Min-Max Scaling
SELECT customer_id,
    (transaction_amount - (SELECT MIN(transaction_amount) FROM transactions)) /
    ((SELECT MAX(transaction_amount) FROM transactions) - (SELECT MIN(transaction_amount) FROM transactions)) AS normalized_transaction
FROM transactions;
```

This would scale the transaction_amount between 0 and 1, making it more suitable for machine learning algorithms.

---

3. SQL for Feature Selection and Dimensionality Reduction

In many real-world datasets, there are too many features, some of which may not be relevant for the problem at hand. Feature selection is a critical step in ML that ensures you're working with the most relevant data. SQL helps by allowing you to focus on the most important features and even reduce the dataset's dimensionality.

- **Selecting Important Features**: SQL can help you identify the most significant features by performing groupings and aggregations.

   Example: If you want to focus on customer activity metrics for churn prediction, you might decide that features such as last_interaction, total_purchases, and account_age are most important. You can use SQL to filter out the less relevant data.

sql
Copy code
```
-- Example: Selecting key features for churn prediction
SELECT customer_id, last_interaction, total_purchases, account_age
FROM customers
```

WHERE is_churned IS NOT NULL;

- **Dimensionality Reduction**: If you have too many features, dimensionality reduction techniques such as Principal Component Analysis (PCA) may be required. While PCA itself is typically done using Python or R, SQL can help reduce the data size and filter out features before running a dimensionality reduction model.

sql
Copy code
-- Example: Selecting top features for PCA (using SQL)
SELECT customer_id, last_interaction, total_purchases
FROM customers
WHERE is_churned IS NOT NULL;

From this selection, you could apply PCA in Python or another environment to reduce the dataset's dimensionality.

---

4. Real-World Example: Preparing Customer Data for a Churn Prediction Model

Let's walk through a real-world example where we use SQL to prepare customer data for a churn prediction model. In this scenario, we aim to predict whether customers will leave a subscription-based service based on various attributes such as account activity, customer demographics, and past interactions.

Step 1: Extract Data from Multiple Tables

First, we extract relevant customer data by joining multiple tables—such as customer information, purchase history, and interaction logs.

sql
Copy code

```sql
-- Example: Extracting relevant features for churn prediction
SELECT  c.customer_id, c.age, c.tenure, c.signup_date, i.last_interaction,
p.total_purchases,
    CASE WHEN c.is_churned = 'Yes' THEN 1 ELSE 0 END AS churn_label
FROM customers c
LEFT JOIN interactions i ON c.customer_id = i.customer_id
LEFT JOIN purchases p ON c.customer_id = p.customer_id
WHERE c.signup_date <= '2020-01-01';
```

In this query, we select features like age, tenure, purchase behavior, and last interaction, while also labeling customers as churned or not churned.

Step 2: Feature Engineering

Next, we apply SQL transformations to generate new features. For example, we create a new feature customer_lifetime_value based on the number of purchases.

sql
Copy code

```sql
-- Example: Creating customer lifetime value (CLV) feature
SELECT customer_id,
    total_purchases * average_purchase_value AS customer_lifetime_value
FROM purchases;
```

This new feature is crucial for understanding the potential value a customer brings to the business, and it can be an important predictor in a churn model.

Step 3: Data Normalization

Normalize data as required for the ML model. For example, normalizing total_purchases and account_age to bring them onto the same scale.

```sql
Copy code
-- Example: Normalizing 'total_purchases' feature
SELECT customer_id,
    (total_purchases - (SELECT MIN(total_purchases) FROM purchases)) /
    ((SELECT MAX(total_purchases) FROM purchases) - (SELECT MIN(total_purchases) FROM purchases)) AS normalized_total_purchases
FROM purchases;
```

SQL plays an essential role in the data preparation pipeline for machine learning. By using SQL for data extraction, feature engineering, and transformation, data scientists can efficiently prepare datasets that are clean, structured, and ready for modeling. SQL also helps streamline the workflow, ensuring that the data fed into machine learning algorithms is both relevant and useful. In this chapter, we've covered how SQL can be used to prepare data for machine learning, from extracting the right data to transforming and normalizing features. The real-world example of churn prediction illustrates how SQL can be a powerful tool in building effective machine learning solutions.

Chapter 23: SQL Best Practices

1. Coding Standards: Writing Readable, Maintainable SQL Code

When working with SQL, especially in collaborative environments or large projects, it's essential to write clean, readable, and maintainable code. Well-structured SQL queries are easier to understand, debug, and modify, making the development process more efficient.

- **Use Meaningful Table and Column Names**: Choose descriptive, intuitive names for tables and columns. Avoid single-letter or vague names, as they make it harder to understand the query's purpose.

  Example: Instead of naming a table t1, name it customer_transactions or orders.

  sql
  Copy code
  ```
  -- Not recommended
  SELECT t1.customer_id, t1.amount FROM t1;


  -- Recommended
  SELECT        customer_id,        transaction_amount        FROM
  customer_transactions;
  ```

- **Consistency in Naming Conventions**: Adopt a consistent naming convention for tables, columns, and aliases. For example, use lowercase letters with underscores to separate words (customer_id, order_date). Avoid mixing naming styles (camelCase, PascalCase, etc.).

sql
Copy code
```
-- Consistent naming convention
SELECT first_name, last_name FROM employees;
```

- **Indentation and Formatting**: Proper indentation and formatting can make complex queries more readable. Indent each clause and subquery properly, and use capital letters for SQL keywords (SELECT, FROM, WHERE, JOIN, etc.).

sql
Copy code
```
-- Example of properly indented SQL query
SELECT customer_id, total_sales
FROM customers
WHERE total_sales > 1000
ORDER BY total_sales DESC;
```

- **Use Aliases for Tables and Columns**: Use clear and concise aliases when querying multiple tables. This enhances readability and avoids confusion when the same table is used multiple times in a query.

sql

Copy code

-- Use aliases for better readability

SELECT c.customer_id, c.name, o.order_date

FROM customers AS c

INNER JOIN orders AS o ON c.customer_id = o.customer_id;

- **Comments**: Comment your SQL code, especially in complex queries. Comments should explain the logic behind tricky sections, why certain functions are used, and how the query fits into the larger project.

sql

Copy code

-- Fetching total sales per customer

SELECT customer_id, SUM(sales_amount) AS total_sales

FROM customer_sales

GROUP BY customer_id;

---

2. Error Handling: Common Pitfalls and Solutions

SQL queries can often lead to errors, especially as they grow more complex. Understanding common pitfalls and how to address them is essential for maintaining smooth development and operations.

- **Handling NULL Values**: NULL values can cause unexpected results in queries. Use COALESCE or IFNULL to handle NULL values and prevent errors from arising.

sql

Copy code

```
-- Handling NULL values
SELECT customer_id, COALESCE(first_name, 'Unknown') AS
first_name
FROM customers;
```

- **Avoiding SQL Injection**: Always use parameterized queries to prevent SQL injection, which can lead to security vulnerabilities.

Example (in Python with SQLAlchemy):

python
Copy code

```python
cursor.execute("SELECT * FROM customers WHERE customer_id =
%s", (customer_id,))
```

Avoid constructing SQL queries directly by concatenating user inputs:

sql
Copy code

```sql
-- Vulnerable code example: Avoid using this pattern!
SELECT * FROM customers WHERE customer_id = " + user_input;
```

- **Dealing with Duplicate Records**: Duplicate records can cause issues when aggregating or filtering data. Use DISTINCT to remove duplicates where appropriate.

sql
Copy code

SQL FOR DATA SCIENCE

```
-- Removing duplicates
SELECT DISTINCT customer_id
FROM orders;
```

- **Performance Pitfalls**: Inefficient queries, especially those involving large datasets, can lead to slow performance. Common performance issues include:

  o **Unindexed Columns**: Queries that involve columns not indexed can be slow, especially when filtering or joining large datasets. Always ensure key columns (e.g., foreign keys) are indexed.

  o **Missing WHERE Clauses**: Always filter data as early as possible to avoid unnecessary full-table scans.

sql

Copy code

```
-- Avoid full-table scans with proper indexing and filtering
SELECT product_id, total_sales
FROM products
WHERE product_category = 'Electronics';
```

- **Transaction Errors**: Transactions are crucial for ensuring data consistency. Make sure you handle ROLLBACK in case of errors to avoid data corruption.

sql

Copy code

```
-- Example: Using transactions and handling errors
BEGIN TRANSACTION;


-- Insert operations
INSERT INTO products (product_id, name) VALUES (101, 'Laptop');


-- If an error occurs, roll back
IF @@ERROR <> 0
BEGIN
   ROLLBACK;
END
ELSE
BEGIN
   COMMIT;
END;
```

---

3. Real-World Example: Code Review for a Team's Analytics Dashboard Project

Let's explore a real-world example of code review for a team's SQL query used in an analytics dashboard project. The goal is to identify best practices and common pitfalls within a query for performance, readability, and maintainability.

Scenario: The team is building an analytics dashboard for an e-commerce website to track sales performance. They have a query that aggregates sales data by product category and region, but the code needs a review to ensure it's efficient and maintainable.

sql

Copy code

```
-- Original Query: Sales Performance by Category and Region
SELECT
    p.product_category,
    r.region,
    SUM(o.sales_amount) AS total_sales,
    COUNT(o.order_id) AS total_orders
FROM
    orders o
INNER JOIN
    products p ON o.product_id = p.product_id
INNER JOIN
    regions r ON o.region_id = r.region_id
WHERE
    o.order_date BETWEEN '2023-01-01' AND '2023-12-31'
GROUP BY
    p.product_category, r.region;
```

Code Review:

1. **Use of Aliases**:
   - The query uses aliases for tables (o, p, and r), which is great. However, using more descriptive aliases could improve readability.

sql

Copy code

```
-- Improved aliases for readability
FROM orders AS o
INNER JOIN products AS p ON o.product_id = p.product_id
```

INNER JOIN regions AS r ON o.region_id = r.region_id

2. **Column and Table Naming**:

- o The column names are clear and meaningful (product_category, region, sales_amount, etc.), which makes the query easy to understand.

3. **WHERE Clause**:

- o The WHERE clause filters orders by date, which is good. However, using date functions like DATE() or DATE_TRUNC() could be more flexible if the date format changes.

4. **Optimization**:

- o **Indexes**: Ensure that columns like order_date, product_id, and region_id are indexed to improve query performance.

- o **Avoiding Redundant Joins**: The query uses multiple joins to get the necessary data, but ensure that only the necessary data is being joined. For instance, if region information is not frequently needed, consider fetching it separately.

sql
Copy code

```
-- Index suggestion for better performance
CREATE INDEX idx_orders_order_date ON orders(order_date);
```

5. **Readability**:

o The query is well-structured, but adding comments to explain the purpose of each section (especially the joins) could make it easier for new team members to understand.

sql

Copy code

-- Aggregating total sales and order count by category and region for 2023
SELECT p.product_category, r.region, SUM(o.sales_amount) AS total_sales, COUNT(o.order_id) AS total_orders

6. **Error Handling**:

   o While not directly applicable in SELECT queries, always ensure to use transactions when performing INSERT, UPDATE, or DELETE operations in a similar context.

SQL best practices are essential for writing efficient, maintainable, and readable code. Whether you're working alone or in a team, following consistent coding standards, handling common errors, and optimizing queries for performance ensures that your SQL code will scale effectively with your data and requirements. In this chapter, we've covered coding standards, error handling, and how to review and improve SQL queries for real-world projects. By implementing these practices, you'll not only write better SQL but also create robust data solutions that are easier to maintain and scale.

Chapter 24: The Future of SQL in Data Science

---

1. SQL's Evolving Role: SQL's Place in Emerging Technologies like AI and IoT

SQL, originally designed for relational database management, has continued to evolve as a critical tool in data science, especially as technologies like Artificial Intelligence (AI), Machine Learning (ML), and the Internet of Things (IoT) grow in significance. While NoSQL databases have become popular for unstructured data, SQL's flexibility, power, and maturity ensure its continued relevance.

- **AI and SQL**: SQL has always been used for extracting and transforming data, the foundational tasks needed for machine learning and AI. With the integration of advanced SQL features like window functions and analytical queries, SQL is a key player in preparing, querying, and manipulating large datasets for AI algorithms.
    - **SQL in Model Training**: SQL can be used to retrieve data in a form that's ready for training machine learning models. As SQL databases support complex joins and aggregations, they make it easier to combine multiple data sources and

transform them into a structured format suitable for model training.

- ○ **SQL for Model Evaluation**: SQL can be used to track model performance metrics stored in relational databases, providing insights into model accuracy, precision, and recall across different segments.

Example: In a recommendation system for an e-commerce platform, SQL can be used to preprocess customer behavior data (e.g., clicks, purchases) before passing it into a machine learning model for product recommendations.

- **IoT and SQL**: The Internet of Things generates a huge volume of time-series data from sensors, devices, and smart applications. SQL databases, particularly those optimized for time-series data (like PostgreSQL with TimescaleDB), are being adapted to efficiently handle real-time data ingestion, storage, and querying.

  - ○ **Real-Time Querying**: SQL allows for the aggregation of real-time sensor data for analytics. In an IoT-enabled factory, SQL can be used to monitor machine performance and detect anomalies based on real-time sensor data.

Example: SQL is used to aggregate and query the temperature, humidity, and vibration data collected from a series of machines in a factory. This data is processed to predict equipment failures and optimize maintenance schedules.

---

2. New SQL Features: Latest Innovations in SQL Databases

As SQL databases adapt to new data management needs, a number of advanced features have been introduced to make them more powerful and suited for the modern data landscape.

- **JSON Support**: Modern SQL databases, like PostgreSQL and MySQL, now offer robust support for JSON data types. This allows SQL to interact with semi-structured data, providing a hybrid model where relational and non-relational data can coexist.

  - **Example**: A retail business can store product reviews, which are semi-structured, as JSON objects inside SQL tables. SQL can then be used to query both structured and unstructured product data.

sql

Copy code

```
-- Querying JSON data in PostgreSQL
SELECT product_name, review->>'text' AS review_text
FROM products
WHERE review->>'rating' = '5';
```

- **SQL for Machine Learning (SQLML)**: Many SQL databases are incorporating machine learning algorithms directly into the database. For example, Microsoft SQL Server and PostgreSQL have introduced extensions for running machine learning algorithms like regression, classification, clustering, and time-series forecasting directly within the SQL environment. This means that data scientists can run models and perform predictions without exporting data to an external ML tool.

  o **Example**: Using SQL-based machine learning algorithms for predicting customer churn, where the SQL database manages both data storage and the training process.

sql
Copy code
```
-- Example of running machine learning algorithm in SQL (SQL Server)
CREATE MODEL churn_model
USING REGRESSION
FROM customer_data
PREDICTING churn;
```

- **Columnar Storage and In-Memory Processing**: To keep up with Big Data demands, modern SQL databases have integrated features like columnar storage and in-memory processing to speed up queries, particularly those involving analytical workloads.

- o **Example**: In a financial analysis scenario, columnar storage helps to perform high-speed aggregations over billions of transactions, dramatically improving query performance in real-time reporting.

- **Distributed SQL**: Databases like Google Spanner and CockroachDB are pushing the boundaries of SQL with distributed architectures that offer the scalability of NoSQL systems while preserving the transactional consistency of traditional SQL.

- o **Example**: A global retailer can use a distributed SQL database to ensure that inventory data is consistent across multiple stores in different regions.

3. Real-World Example: Using SQL in Future-Proof Data Architectures

The role of SQL in future-proof data architectures is becoming more vital as the volume, variety, and velocity of data grow. Organizations are increasingly using SQL to create integrated data environments that can handle diverse workloads, from transactional operations to advanced analytics.

- **Multi-Cloud Data Management**: SQL-based cloud data warehouses like Google BigQuery and Amazon Redshift are at the heart of modern data architectures. These cloud platforms combine the scalability of distributed systems with SQL's structured query capabilities, making them the backbone for analytics in large organizations.

Example: A multinational bank uses a cloud-based SQL data warehouse to combine transaction data from multiple branches worldwide. SQL is used to aggregate transaction volumes, detect fraud patterns, and generate real-time business insights.

sql

Copy code

```
-- Querying for unusual transaction amounts across all branches in a
bank's cloud data warehouse
SELECT branch_id, transaction_id, amount
FROM transactions
WHERE amount > 1000000;
```

- **Data Lakes and SQL**: Data lakes, which store large volumes of unstructured or semi-structured data, are often paired with SQL to bridge the gap between raw data storage and actionable insights. SQL can be used for ETL (Extract, Transform, Load) processes, cleaning and transforming data as it moves between the data lake and structured data systems.

Example: A healthcare company stores patient data, medical records, and research notes in a data lake. SQL is then used to perform data extraction and transformation tasks, preparing the data for detailed analysis, reporting, and machine learning.

sql
Copy code
```
-- SQL to extract and transform data from a data lake for analysis
SELECT patient_id, diagnosis, COUNT(*) AS visits
FROM data_lake.patient_data
GROUP BY patient_id, diagnosis;
```

- **IoT and Real-Time Analytics**: SQL's ability to handle real-time data from IoT devices is another critical feature for future-proof architectures. As more businesses adopt IoT sensors and devices, SQL remains a central tool for analyzing and aggregating data on the fly.

Example: In a smart city project, SQL databases process real-time traffic sensor data to monitor vehicle flow, control traffic lights, and predict congestion, all while ensuring data consistency across multiple sources.

sql
Copy code
```
-- Query to analyze traffic data in a smart city project
SELECT intersection_id, AVG(traffic_flow) AS avg_flow
FROM traffic_sensors
```

```
WHERE timestamp > CURRENT_TIMESTAMP - INTERVAL 1
HOUR
GROUP BY intersection_id;
```

: SQL's Future in Data Science

SQL continues to evolve, adapting to the increasing complexity of data science, big data, and emerging technologies like AI and IoT. The combination of SQL's powerful querying capabilities with modern innovations in cloud computing, machine learning, and real-time data processing makes it an indispensable tool for data scientists today and in the future.

As businesses look to leverage more advanced data architectures, SQL will remain at the heart of the most robust data solutions, enabling data-driven decision-making at scale. The introduction of new features, such as JSON support, machine learning extensions, and distributed SQL databases, ensures that SQL remains a relevant and indispensable technology in the ever-evolving landscape of data science.

In the years ahead, SQL will continue to evolve, maintaining its role as the backbone for data storage, querying, and analysis, while also integrating seamlessly with the technologies of tomorrow.